The fascination of life aboard a sailing-ship is partly that of a small, self-contained world. When one of the few surviving wind-jammers sets out on a voyage, she becomes a completely isolated speck on the ocean. She carries no wireless, keeps far from most steamship tracks, and may not even sight land for from three to five months; she thus becomes a little world of her own, solely dependent on the weather, and on the skill and strength of her people. This book is the story of a recent voyage, in a modern four-masted barque, from Australia to Falmouth, round Cape Horn, recording the daily and nightly life on board, the creatures seen in the stormy southern ocean and in the Tropics. Enough is said about the handling of a big sailing-ship to fill in some of the gaps left by other recent books on the subject. And never has the undying beauty of sail been better brought out than in the author's photographs.

WHITE SAILS CROWD- ING

BY

COMMANDER

C. M. BUTLIN

D.S.C., R.N.

JONATHAN CAPE
30 BEDFORD SQUARE
LONDON

FIRST PUBLISHED 1935
JONATHAN CAPE LTD.   30 BEDFORD SQUARE, LONDON
AND 91 WELLINGTON STREET WEST, TORONTO

794.1.

PRINTED IN GREAT BRITAIN IN THE CITY OF OXFORD
AT THE ALDEN PRESS
PAPER MADE BY JOHN DICKINSON & CO., LTD.
BOUND BY A. W. BAIN & CO. LTD.

CONTENTS

I	THE SHIP	15
II	THE START AND FIRST TWELVE DAYS	21
III	ABOUT MARIEHAMN AND CARGOES	29
IV	STORM, ISLANDS AND NAVIGATION	38
V	ON MEALS AND THE COOK	49
VI	THE CREW	54
VII	CALM	65
VIII	ALBATROSSES, PETRELS AND PRIONS	72
IX	CAPE HORN AND TIERRA DEL FUEGO	78
X	MORE CALM	88
XI	EASTER AT SEA	98
XII	A SAILING SHIP'S RIGGING — TACKING SHIP	103
XIII	THE CAPTAIN, PERCY GRAINGER AND THE MATE	111
XIV	PHOSPHORESCENCE, WHALES AND WATERSPOUT	120
XV	MODELS, CRAFTS, AND BOOKS	127
XVI	TAKEN ABACK AND CHANGING SAILS	135
XVII	SAILMAKER AND THIRD MATE	144
XVIII	SOUTH-EAST TRADES	151
XIX	DOLDRUMS, SHARK, SUCKER FISH, STEAMERS	159
XX	THE LINE	173
XXI	NORTH-EAST TRADES	181
XXII	NEAR THE TROPIC OF CANCER	188

CONTENTS

XXIII   SARGASSO SEA, STEAMERS, FISH   199

XXIV   TRAINING IN SAIL   216

XXV   IN THE WESTERLIES   226

XXVI   A DOLPHIN, NEWS, AND SAILING-SHIPS'
       CHARTERS   233

XXVII   THE END OF THE VOYAGE   244

BIBLIOGRAPHY   255

ILLUSTRATIONS

ROLLING HOME   *frontispiece*

'L'AVENIR' LEAVING SPENCER GULF   *facing p.* 22

CLOSE-HAULED IN A FRESH BREEZE   22

LOOKING AFT FROM THE FORECASTLE-HEAD   26

A GALE IN THE SOUTHERN OCEAN   ~~38~~ 42

RUNNING BEFORE A GALE   44

LOOKING FOR THE SUN   60

THE WATCH WORKING ON A YARD   60

SECOND MATE HOLDING ALBATROSS   74

WHITE SAILS AND TRACERY OF RIGGING   106

THE CAPTAIN, HOLDING FRASSIE, WITH THE MATE   116

AT WORK ALOFT IN FINE WEATHER   138

ON A YARD-ARM, ABOVE THE SHIMMERING SEA   142

ACROBATICS ON A YARD-ARM   176

BENDING ON AN OLD SAIL   188

CHANGING SAILS ON THE FOREMAST   220

A STRUGGLE ON A YARD-ARM   232

ASTRIDE THE END OF A TOPGALLANT YARD-ARM   232

'LAND IN SIGHT'   246

To My Wife
Who Shared the Adventure
and to Eve and Teddy
Who Launched Us Upon It

WHITE SAILS CROWDING

CHAPTER I

THE SHIP

'THERE she is.'

As the car came over a crest of a rise, the late afternoon sun made the waters of the Spencer Gulf into a shining strip of silver against which were silhouetted the tapering masts of our ship, looking very tiny in the far distance.

This was near the end of the first stage of our journey from Sydney to England via Cape Horn. We had come from Adelaide by road through miles of wheat country, which was especially appropriate as we were to travel on top of 46,000 bags of wheat from these districts. The noon temperature had been over 115° F. and the glare from the stripped and parched-looking fields had been almost blinding. The country is mostly wide rolling plain, and as all fences are of wire there is nothing special to catch one's eye beyond a few scattered homesteads, with perhaps a tree or two to shade them.

There was little traffic except for an occasional empty wagon drawn by a team of eight horses, four abreast, returning from the nearest wheat depot. At these depots, the bags are stacked into enormous rectangular piles perhaps twenty feet high; usually they are not covered over, for at this time of year rain is almost impossible in South Australia. From the inland ones the wheat is transported by rail to the most convenient seaport: in some of the smaller ports the farmers not only bring the wheat down to the jetty but themselves help to load it into the ketches which take it off to some ship at anchor off the coast.

As we approached Port Germein where *L'Avenir* was lying at the end of the longest jetty in South Australia, we saw that there was another sailing ship behind her and a third at anchor near by. These proved to be the three-masted barque *Winterhude* and the four-masted barquentine *Mozart*.

The township consists of an hotel, a few weather-board cottages and most important, huge stacks of wheat which have the air of dominating the place. It is not connected to any railway system, but a track runs from the dump to the end of the pier a mile and a half away, where the water is deep enough for ships to lie alongside.

As it was after working hours when we arrived, the ancient railway engine had stopped for the day, so we wearily trudged down the jetty with some of our belongings, and climbed on board feeling rather like emigrants. The captain's welcome soon dispelled this, and when the young steward showed us our cabins and asked naïvely with a charming smile, 'Do you like it?' we could truthfully answer, 'Very much'. *L'Avenir* was built as a training ship for Belgian cadets and we had been given the 2nd and 3rd lieutenants' cabins which had good solid mahogany drawers under the bunks and plenty of hanging space. Next door was the pantry and opposite on the other side of a passage was the dining saloon, which was formerly the wardroom.

The ship remained alongside the jetty for a few days which gave an opportunity for checking stores. Much thought and preparation were behind us, as four to five months of voyaging out of reach of any shop demanded that we should be entirely self-contained, except for the main items of food which would be provided on board. Although it was desperately hot there was plenty to do, and final lists of death-bed repentances grew with alarming rapidity. Such items as Bovril, barley sugar, hammock rings, fretsaw blades, fly-papers, and spare torch batteries, made one feel that there was no limit to the extra stuff that it might be wise to have. We had also to collect our seaboots and oilskins, which seemed slightly ridiculous during a heat wave.

Though the iron sides of the ship held the heat for most of the night, the evenings came as a real relief, for there was bound to be some movement of air on deck. With all due respect to this part of Australia it has much in common with deserts, for nearly always the sun rises and sets with the most amazing beauty. Sometimes the colours are almost harshly vivid; at others they are so delicate that they cause a dull ache of longing for the unknown.

A few details of *L'Avenir* may be of interest.

She is a steel 4-masted barque, built by Rickmers of Bremerhaven in 1908 for the Association Maritime Belge as a training ship for 75 to 100 cadets.

Length	313 ft. (with jibboom 346 ft.)
Beam	45 ft.
Draft, fully loaded	24 ft.
Sail area	31,000 sq. ft., about
Cargo capacity	3,400 tons
Displacement loaded	5,700 tons, about

Minimum ballast for sailing, 1,600 tons.

Masts of steel with lower masts and top masts in one piece, and with fidded topgallant masts.

From main truck to keel 192 ft.

Length of lower yards, 90 ft. Weight 5 tons each. All yards of steel except royals, which are wooden spars 45 ft. long.

L'Avenir was bought by Captain Gustaf Eriksson and made her first voyage under the Finnish flag in 1932.

When we arrived on board, *L'Avenir* still required two days to complete loading. The wheat was brought down in trucks hauled by the old locomotive, whose driver also combined the duties of harbour master and pilot; stevedores loaded it into the holds. Wheat is always loaded into a sailing ship in bags, for if she were to remain listed over on one tack, for two or three weeks at a time, there would be danger of a cargo in bulk shifting.

As a wheat cargo is light, there is always difficulty in getting a ship down to her Plimsoll marks so that a certain number of the bags, perhaps 1000, are opened in order that the grain can fill up the spaces between the bags. It is fascinating to watch a heap of it trickling down a small hole like sand in an hour glass.

As a rule, the work is much easier for the stevedores if a lot of bags are cut, for then the level of the wheat will be lower, and it may not be necessary to push sacks into awkward corners under deck beams right out at the ship's side. In some ports the stevedores adopt the low trick of carrying a small blade, sharp as a razor, fastened to a ring which is worn on a middle finger. When each bag is in position, a final affectionate stroke will make a slit down the side so neatly that even the most watchful mate is often unable to detect it. In the past Adelaide has earned a bad name in this direction. While *L'Avenir* was unloading at Avonmouth a large wheat steamer, which was discharging near her, found that 10,000 bags had been slashed. As the ship has to pay 9d. for every bag damaged, it is needless to add that the chief mate of the steamer lost his job.

During the last few days of loading, the crew were employed in bending the sails, for while *L'Avenir* had been in harbour, the sails had been stowed down in the sail locker. Directly all the cargo was in, a tug from

Port Pirie towed us out about three miles from the jetty, to an anchorage from which we could sail whenever there should be a fair breeze.

Before we could leave Australia, the captain had to go over to Port Pirie, ten miles away, to get the clearance papers from the customs authorities, and to fire a final broadside at the ship chandler whose poor memory caused us to go short of a few much-needed commodities. The captain went over in the ship's motor boat, and on the way back gave a passage to an English lad, belonging to *Winterhude*, who had just come out of hospital. This boy had been sitting astride the extreme end of a yardarm, outside the lifts, sheets, and clewlines, hauling on some rope which gave so suddenly that he fell off backwards. Happily he was over the water, but he passed so close to the ship's side that one arm was broken by striking the plating.

The captain had landed looking very smart, and wearing a stiff collar in spite of the heat wave. After leaving the sweltering streets and wharfs of Port Pirie, he celebrated the final severance from shore affairs and their worries with a magnificent gesture. Taking off the now moist and crumpled collar, he flung it into the sea, beaming with satisfaction and relief.

The ship was ready to sail with the first fair wind.

CHAPTER II

THE START AND FIRST TWELVE DAYS

'If this breeze holds we shall be in deep water by eight.'

The pilot's words broke hazily through sleep. But though it was only 3 a.m., the sounds of many feet on deck above us soon had a rousing effect.

Though it was still moonlit night, everyone was busy. Aloft on each mast were a few men casting off. the gaskets from the sails, leaving them struggling noisily in the breeze to free themselves from confining buntlines and clewlines. The rest of the crew were toiling round the capstan to weigh the anchor. For though there is a donkey boiler, coal is too expensive an item for steam to be kept day after day while waiting for a fair wind.

Directly the anchor was clear of the ground, the head-sails were hoisted and with the fore lower top-gallant sail sheeted and aback, the ship turned slowly round. As soon as she was heading towards the channel every sail was set. In the semi-darkness it was a scene of ordered confusion — sharp orders from the captain and mates, the rush of feet, some of them in clogs, and the hoarse shouts of the sailmaker as he gave the time for the men hauling behind him — all this combined to make a most vivid impression. Gradually the sky over the dark hills became paler, until at length the light of dawn tinted the upper sails a delicate pink. When should we next see the sun rise over the land?

The pilot's remark proved true, for by 8 o'clock he had taken a last-minute mail, was shaking hands warmly with everyone in sight and, after wishing us a good voyage, started back to Port Pirie in his heavy-looking motor boat. As it became a speck in the distance we really felt that the last link with the land had been cleanly severed.

Rare and precious in the Spencer Gulf in summer, the northerly breeze held all day with varying strength. It was very hot and the ship's course down the centre of the gulf brought us just in sight of Port Broughton and Wallaroo, at each of which could be seen the masts of two sailing ships, distorted by mirage.

During the night and the following day, except for a few hours' calm, there was enough northerly breeze to keep the ship moving down the gulf. It was a broiling day and longing eyes rested on the sandy beaches in the distance, wondering when would come the next opportunity for surfing. The Islands at the entrance to the Spencer Gulf break up the swell too much to give good surf on these beaches, which should otherwise be perfect, as they are said to be fairly safe from sharks. Though while *L'Avenir* was lying at Port

top: *L'Avenir* leaving the Spencer Gulf
bottom: Close-hauled in a fresh breeze. Looking aft

Germein pier, the ugly black dorsal fin of a shark could often be seen cruising in the offing. This very afternoon a small hammer-headed shark passed underneath the stern, looking ridiculously improbable.

During the afternoon a ship was sighted right astern. After an hour she was made out to be a barque and though there were many conjectures as to who it might be, it was only too obvious that we should soon know, as she was overhauling us steadily. As we had every sail set, and as they were trimmed correctly in the light of experience and theory, we could only curse the barnacles which coated our bottom and checked our speed. At dusk she passed close to us going at least a knot faster. Signalling with Morse lamp at length gave way to a megaphone conversation between the captains. She was *Killoran*, also belonging to Captain Gustaf Eriksson, and she had that day sailed from Port Victoria. Her sails made a beautifully graceful silhouette against the late evening sky. A warm glow of light came out from the midship deckhouse. She was able to give us the latest news of some of the other grain ships. The *Viking* had sailed two days before but had been forced to anchor for a time somewhere in the Gulf to wait for northerly wind. The two German ships *Priwall* and *Padua* were ready to sail.

As *Killoran* was disappearing into the darkness ahead, one of the Adelaide Gulf steamers, blazing with lights, passed close to our stern on her way from Port Lincoln. There was much Morse flashing and her

'Bon voyage' was to be the last message from the outside world for many weeks. As her lights grew fainter, it was difficult not to feel a little forlorn as we moved slowly out towards the open and very empty sea.

We had at least been lucky in getting out of the Spencer Gulf, for ships have been known to take three weeks to do so, being forced to drop anchor every time the wind dropped or headed them.

The prospect of a long voyage has one advantage, in that it makes it seem worth while to unpack a good deal and to arrange all household gods comfortably and conveniently. With books, a picture or two, calendars, cushions, and a few yards of bright chintz, our cabins soon had a homely appearance. Though that of course was before the ship began to heel over.

A heavy south-westerly swell and a westerly wind made it reasonably certain that we should follow the Cape Horn route. It is the wind met with during the first week of the voyage which decides sailing ship captains which way to go home. Though westerly winds are normal south of Australia, there is occasionally a spell of easterly weather, and if this holds long enough for a ship to get clear to the westward of the continent, she will pick up the SE. trades which will give her a chance of making a good passage round the Cape of Good Hope. It is a unique state of affairs to leave Australia with a completely open mind as to which way round the world one is going to sail.

As we were steering south, it seemed wise to make full use of every scrap of sunshine before it became too feeble to be of use. It was while we were sitting aft, that we suddenly noticed an unfamiliar figure standing dejectedly by the chart house. Small and miserable looking, he was dressed in slouch cap, coat and trousers many sizes too large for him, and sand shoes which may once have been white. Underneath dirt, and a ten days' growth of beard, his face showed pale. In a moment the news spread through the ship that a stowaway had been found. We could not help feeling sorry for him as he was led down to have his first interview with the large and wrathful captain. For with a full crew an extra mouth to feed would not be likely to please the owner when he came to hear about it. The stowaway had been hiding in the forepeak for over a week. He had come on board on the Friday evening before the ship was towed out from the jetty; we had sailed on Wednesday and this was Saturday. The captain remarked to us that at least the crew would be pleased, as they would no longer have to clean out the pig sties. The captain told us that, while in Australia, he had received letters from all over the continent from people of all classes and of both sexes imploring him to let them sign on in any capacity. Adventure and the romance of these last of the sailing ships seemed to be the main motives. There may be others: a girl from Port Victoria wrote that she was strong, willing and just twenty.

She enclosed her photograph and everyone who looked at it whistled.

It had been interesting to note the reactions of our friends to the news that we were travelling home in a wind-jammer. 'You are mad', was one of the immediate comments, but it was rare that we came across any attitude between that and extreme envy. The objections raised were manifold, such as Cape Horn weather, lack of fresh food, shortage of fresh water, restricted company, cramped accommodation and unsheltered deck. But above all, the length of the voyage, three months at the very least and possibly over four. Fortunately we were in no great hurry. As for the other disadvantages, most of them proved to be phantoms when we were able to gather reliable information about the conditions on board. Actually we had erred on the side of being over-prepared, having brought blankets and rugs, fresh and tinned fruit, luxuries such as chocolate, biscuits, and nuts. Sufficient changes of clothes to solve the laundry problem, a case full of stuff from the chemist, a fair selection of tools, materials for sewing, knitting and making hammocks, and most important, a quantity of books—Dickens, Scott and other classics that get squeezed out by the speed of modern life, Conrad, C. E. Montague, Mottram, some anthologies, and various odds and ends bought from the second-hand stalls of most of the big cities in Australia, with a collection of old *Blackwoods* and journals of different

26

[*facing:* Looking aft from the forecastle-head, showing triangular mainsail and cross-

sorts. We soon adapted ourselves to the new existence and never found the time hang heavily. If it had, the sailmaker was usually able to provide work on old sails.

The captain had decided to run the easting down in 51° S. or 52° S. until within a few hundred miles of the coast of South America, when he would go down to 60° S. for rounding Cape Horn. This is 1100 miles more than the shortest, or Great Circle track, from Australia to Cape Horn, which would go down to 78° S., only 12° from the South Pole. Some authorities recommend a composite track along the parallel of 60° S., but in 1933, the *Herzogin Cecilie* found so much ice in 56° S. that she was forced to come north again, wasting some precious time in doing so.

On the 9th day out the advantage was taken of the ship being fairly steady to hoist in and secure the anchors. The lack of a fiddler or a shanty man must have been felt by the watch as they trudged round and round the capstan. The anchors were bolted down, lashed with wire rope and wedged between bollards in such a way that the ship could have turned turtle without fear of them shifting a fraction of an inch.

A party under the carpenter spent some time making sure of the cargo hatches, which are as vital to a ship's safety as arteries are to the human body. The fore hatch in the well-deck needed and got most attention as it would get the worst buffeting and might be under water frequently. The usual securings for the hatch are a tarpaulin cover stretched tightly on top of the stout boards which rest on cross beams. Across the top of this are two iron bars of H section kept down by large butterfly screws at each end. For the southern ocean, the whole fore hatch is encased in the heaviest timber available, and the ends of the final cross baulks are fastened down with more long screws.

It must be admitted with shame that as early as the 12th day, while talking about our probable destination, we sank to the discussion of what we would order for our first meal ashore. . . .

On the 13th day we passed a piece of floating timber, and wondered when we should next see anything belonging to land.

CHAPTER III

ABOUT MARIEHAMN AND CARGOES

ONE evening shortly before sailing we had been fortunate in being invited to the captain's cabin to meet the captains of *Winterhude* and *Mozart*, for it gave us the opportunity of learning more about that fascinating place, Mariehamn. Though there is only a village there, it must be one of the most romantic ports in the world, for it is the home of the only real fleet of deep water sailing ships still in existence.

Mariehamn, with its beautiful harbour, is in the Aaland Islands, which lie at the entrance to the Gulf of Bothnia, slightly nearer Sweden than Finland. About 100 years ago Russia took the Aaland Islands from Sweden. But time did not weaken allegiance, for when the Baltic States were formed in 1918 the Aaland Islanders did their best to be returned to Sweden. But the Great Powers thought otherwise. Perhaps from lack of knowledge of history or geography, or else from mere expedience, it was decided that they must be a part of Finland. They are however self-governing, and no Finnish forces are allowed to use the islands, whose safety is guaranteed by the Great Powers. The inhabitants are exempt from military service. No Finn may buy land until he has lived five years on the islands.

Even now very few of the inhabitants can speak Finnish, a language which is changing rapidly due to the efforts being made to supersede the Swedish words which used to abound. It is said that a Finn who has been out of the country for a few years finds it most difficult to talk correctly.

True Finns are of Mongolian origin and some of those in the crew were regarded as being rather savages by the Swedish Finns, who say that they are liable to whip out a knife in a fight or when annoyed.

There are about forty ocean going sailing ships still in commission, of which some sixteen are training ships for the navies or mercantile marines of Foreign Powers. Of the remaining cargo carriers, Captain Gustaf Eriksson of Mariehamn owns fourteen, and runs them with wonderful efficiency in spite of the depression and the keen competition of steamers. His crews are assured by the fact that Finland and other Scandinavian countries insist on sailing ship experience for candidates for mate's tickets.

As a rule his ships leave Europe in September or October, and now, owing to exchange and tariff in Australia, they go out in ballast with no certainty of getting a charter for the return voyage. Each captain has his own ideas as to the best route, and guards them jealously. Usually the wind decides whether the start shall be by the English Channel or North of the

Orkneys. Usually the tracks followed lie to the west-ward of Madeira, between Africa and Cape Verde Islands, across the Equator in about 15° W., after which the SE. trades may force ships to within 100 miles of the coast of South America near Pernambuco. Then they work south until they reach the westerlies, when they will make well to the southward of the Cape of Good Hope, perhaps sighting Tristan da Cunha and some icebergs on the way, until at last they reach the Roaring Forties which will take them across to Australia.

A very brief description of the wind systems which make these voyages possible may not be out of place. The prevailing winds in the North Atlantic are westerly. In the tropics north of the Equator are the NE. trades, or passage winds, which blow with remarkable regularity in both strength and direction, although the north and south limits vary somewhat. In the tropics south of the line, there are the SE. trades which share the same characteristics as the NE. ones. In the southern ocean westerly winds blow right round the world, generally being found to be stronger the further south one goes. Between the trades and again between them and the westerlies lie belts of variable winds and calms which may prove difficult for a sailing ship to get through.

On arrival in Australian waters Captain Eriksson's ships make for Port Lincoln or Port Victoria, both of them in the Spencer Gulf, where they wait for orders.

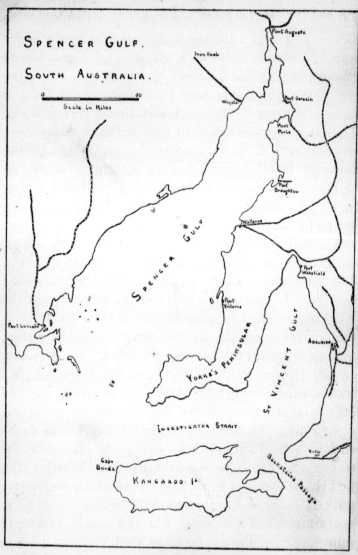

Map showing Adelaide and the Spencer Gulf. Sailing ships call at Port Lincoln or Port Victoria for orders and may load there or at Wallaroo, Port Broughton, Port Germein or Port Augusta

At the beginning of 1934 no less than ten sailing ships arrived at Port Victoria within twenty-four hours. Seven ships anchored between 2 p.m. and dusk and the remaining three early the following morning. This must be a record for a great number of years for any harbour in the world.

Directly the ship arrives, if a charter has been arranged for her she will at once sail to the loading port, which will be in the Spencer Gulf, unless it is Adelaide. There are jetties at most of the loading places except Port Victoria and Port Broughton where the wheat is brought off in ketches. Many of the ships have water ballast tanks which have large lids so that they can also be used for cargo; the remainder carry up to 1700 tons of sand which must be jettisoned in deep water. Not all can be thrown overboard at once, for a ship with sand ballast would capsize if completely empty. So a few hundred tons, called 'stiffening', are kept in one hold until enough cargo has been embarked in the others to make her stable.

The 1934 charters were about 24s. 6d. a ton, which represents the total earnings of a ship for a year. The expenses are heavy, for the ship must pay harbour dues, towage, pilot's fees and also for loading and unloading. All these charges vary according to the port and half of them cannot be estimated until the unloading port is known, after the ship's arrival at Falmouth or Queenstown. At Port Germein, the loading alone cost about 2s. 6d. a ton. In some ports such as Port Augusta, at the head of the Spencer Gulf, and of course London, there is a very heavy bill to pay for tugs. Cargoes are insured, and also the crews and their effects, but Captain Eriksson does not insure the ships themselves, as the total premiums would be equivalent to losing a ship a year.

If any member of the crew deserts in Australia, the ship is fined £100; therefore the owner will not sign on anyone without a deposit of that amount, or at least a guarantee. The time taken to load in Australia varies from three to six weeks according to the facilities of the Port, and then the ships sail immediately there is a fair wind. After unloading in Europe, the usual practice is for them to return to Mariehamn, pay off the crew, and remain for a month or two until it is time to sign on a fresh crew and start the next voyage. Sometimes if a ship is late arriving in Europe, she may remain at the unloading port until the time comes for her to sail for Australia, but only if the harbour dues are reasonable.

A wheat cargo is fairly light, and unless it is very well trimmed the ship does not come down to her loading marks even with the hatches filled up to the very top of the coamings. Ships that carry water ballast will of course use their ballast tanks for wheat, although the loading and unloading of it is not very convenient.

A heavy cargo, such as saltpetre, requires special

stowing, for if it was all put into the bottom of the ship, it would make her so stiff that she would roll her masts out. Therefore two-thirds of the cargo is heaped along the length of the main hold in triangular cross section, while the rest is loaded into the between decks. After it has been on board a few days, saltpetre sets hard, so that no amount of rolling will make it shift. When the time comes to unload it, it can only be broken out with crowbars.

The appearance of a ship on her beam-ends at an angle of 70 degrees

If there should be any danger of cargo or ballast shifting, heavy boards are placed fore and aft in the hold much after the principle of groins on the sea-shore. One year this precaution was omitted in *Herzogin Cecilie* while she was in sand ballast. Struck by a very heavy squall, she heeled so far over that suddenly there was a rumbling sound and a sickening lurch as all the sand avalanched down to the lee side. It must have been a ghastly moment for those on

35

board when they realized that she was not going to right herself. She lay over at an angle of 70° with the lower sides of the hatches several feet under water. For a few minutes they must have thought they were doomed. Then the light of hope filled their eyes as they saw that the hatch covers were standing up against the wash of the swirling waters.

All the sheets were let go and the sails blew themselves to pieces. Then everyone went down into the hold and began shifting back the ballast quite literally for their lives. Most fortunately there was on board a lot of timber which was to have been used during the voyage to replace the worn out poop deck. These planks were placed fore and aft along the upper sides of the three rows of stanchions supporting the between decks, so as to form a series of three steps. The sand was then shovelled up from step to step. Except for a flickering light or two, the hold was in darkness and as the men toiled, they expected that at any moment the hatch covers would give in and that the sea would come pouring down from above. It was as terrifying as being trapped in a submarine, for there was no hope for anyone if the hatches gave and the ship sank. With such a list it would have been impossible to get out the weather or upper boats, while everything on the lee side had been swept away: boats, davits, bulwarks, and rails had all disappeared.

Had the men come on deck, the scene of confusion there with the topgallant yardarms sometimes touching the water would have been far less comforting than the sight of the men working superhumanly in the hold. At first almost imperceptibly as the heaps on the steps grew, the list began to decrease. But this was not the end of their danger. For after many hours' work there was a sudden rending and crashing sound as the planks broke under the strain, and all the sand slithered down in a second avalanche until the list was almost as bad as ever. Mercifully no one was buried, and directly yet more planks had been built up on the stanchions, the labour continued once more. Except for short spells snatched for a meal there was no rest. To get forward on deck, the only way was to walk on the ship's side. In the saloon they ate their food on the side bulkhead.

At the end of forty-eight hours of ceaseless struggle the ship was more or less upright, and undaunted by the scene of wreckage, work aloft was next taken in hand. Most of the braces had carried away which allowed the heavy yards to swing uncontrolled in the swell, so that most of the crance irons securing them to the masts were fractured or damaged. All the spare ones were sent up and the others were lashed with wire until they were more or less serviceable. Another suit of sails was sent up and *Herzogin Cecilie* continued her voyage to Australia instead of struggling into the nearest harbour to recuperate. It was only the fact that she had six hundred tons of water ballast in deep tanks which prevented her from going right over when the sand shifted.

CHAPTER IV

STORM, ISLANDS AND NAVIGATION

ON the fourteenth day the glass began to fall ominously and hard squalls with rain left no doubt that we were in for a blow. Except to snatch a quick meal, the captain remained on deck, spending most of the time looking aloft at the sails and rigging, or else astern at the rising seas as if to gauge the weight of wind behind them. Throughout the ship there was a feeling of tense excitement.

The wind had been freshening all the afternoon and by dusk the ship was doing twelve knots with a gale on the starboard quarter; this must have been about her maximum speed heavily loaded as she was, and with a thick growth of weeds and barnacles on her bottom. Heavy planks had been placed round the skylights to protect the glass and over the whole canvas was lashed.

By 9 p.m. the squalls were coming with such fierce strength that the watch was ordered to furl the royals, the highest sails on each mast. Beginning from aft with the mizen, while the mate lowered the halyard, the whole watch manned the clewlines and buntlines so that as each yard came down, the foot of the sail was confined to it at its corners, and in four places along its length, leaving balloons of struggling canvas between each. Immediately the main and fore royals had been dealt with in turn, the watch was split up, two or three being sent aloft on each mast to stow the sails. Once aloft, the boys were completely isolated, for no human voice could hope to vie with the shrieking wind. It was bitterly cold, and the boys looked like specks as they fought with the bellying canvas on the swaying yards to pass the gaskets round sail and yard, so that there should be nothing for the wind to catch. The ship listed over so far that it was impossible to walk without clutching some support.

As the night went on, the sounds heard from between decks became terrifying, at least to unaccustomed ears. The following seas were chasing each other along the ship's side with a rush and a roar, with often a thud followed by a streaming sound as their crests flopped on deck. The ship creaked and groaned as if in torture, while everything in cabins became very much alive; even heavy drawers would slide out if left unlocked. Whenever a sea hit the midship deckhouse, enough came past the closed door to form a noisy cascade down the ladder and to flood the lee cabins near its foot.

At midnight, the usual time for the watch to change, all hands were required to shorten sail down to lower topsails and fore and main courses. The fore upper topgallant did not give in without a struggle, for while it was being clewed up, all the new wire buntlines parted, and the sail behaved like a balloon gone mad. A hawser had to be passed round it and the end brought to a capstan so that the middle of the refractory sail was gathered up under the yard. Even then it took most of both watches up on the yard to smother it and to pass the gaskets. Besides a little damage to the clews of the sail, the crance iron, the metal ring which keeps the yard from blowing away from the mast, was fractured. Wet and cold, the watch below only had an hour in the forecastle before coming on watch again at 4 a.m.

To those who enjoy heights, it may seem that going aloft is easy enough; and so it is to any active boy in nice weather. But it must be remembered that sail is only taken in when it is blowing too hard for it to be carried in safety. The strain on the rigging alone is so painfully obvious that it is best not to think about it. The temperature during that part of the voyage during which bad weather is most likely is only a few degrees above freezing point, and frequent squalls of rain and hail will numb even the hardiest hands. The enthusiastic rock climber should bear this in mind, he may have tackled a difficult face in a blizzard, but at least the rocks have been fixed. Imagine the effect of such a lurch as will make cabin drawers slide out, on a boy out on a royal yard wrestling with stiff, wet and heavy canvas. As the ship rolls over to leeward the sensation is like going down in an express lift and then stopping too suddenly. At the extreme of the roll, instead of being horizontal, the yard will of course be sloping steeply down towards the raging sea below and the ship will give a sort of shake, as if to rid herself of the puny creatures aloft before she starts her upward motion. The old saying 'One hand for the ship and one for yourself' is all very well, but there are times when both hands must be used on the job; then, when a moment of danger comes unexpectedly, there is a swift clutch for a safe hold. Happily accidents are not very common, not from lack of danger but because of the wonderful activity, quickness and sense of balance that a sailing ship teaches.

That the captain is definitely anxious while the men are aloft shortening a sail is no sign of weakness. On this night he was on deck until six the following morning. A grey comfortless dawn with an angry rising sea showed the haggard faces of the wet and weary crew; the after end of the poop and the forecastle head were the only dry places on deck. Greybeards came chasing after the ship and got within a few inches of the edge of the poop deck, but always her stern rose before they could climb on board.

All day it blew hard and two men were required at the wheel. Under such conditions, in some of the ships with higher-geared steering wheels, almost the whole watch would be needed to keep her steady on her course; big following seas striking the rudder exert an enormous force. Sometimes a wheel takes charge and lifts the helmsman off his feet and carries him over the top to the other side.

During a storm, one of the most important problems for the captain to decide is how long it is safe to continue running before it. While making ten or twelve knots in the right direction, the natural tendency is to hold on, rather than to heave-to and waste time, during which several hundred miles might have been covered. But there may come a time when wind and sea have increased to such an extent that the ship is almost unmanageable and is in danger of broaching-to. Broaching-to usually ends in disaster, for it happens when a sea, overcoming the effect of the rudder, throws the ship's stern one way or the other so that she comes round broadside on to the sea, with probably more sail than she can stand and eventually gets the wind on the fore side of the sails, all the time being buried in the sea due to her speed. If heaving-to is left until too late, it may be almost as dangerous as broaching-to.

As soon as it is decided that the ship must be hove to the sail is reduced to the fore, or to the fore and main lower topsails, and the storm spanker is got ready for setting. Then all the yards are braced round as sharp as they will come. The ship is kept running dead before the wind until a favourable moment comes, perhaps after a particularly heavy sea has passed or

[*facing:* A gale in the Southern Ocean. Two men at the w]

during a momentary easing of the wind. Then the wheel is put up, the storm spanker is set, and everyone holds on like grim death until the critical period is over. The ship will come round and will behave like a half-tide rock until she has lost most of her speed. Then the wheel is lashed hard up and the ship will lie $6\frac{1}{2}$ points off the wind, drifting sideways with neither head nor stern way. Should she still keep head way all sail can be taken off her if necessary, for the windage of the yards, if braced up sharp, is equivalent to at least one topsail, and will be sufficient to prevent her from gathering stern way.

In a long ship which steers well and has only a short well deck, as in *L'Avenir*, it should rarely be necessary to heave-to. This particular gale caused no special anxiety as the sea had not reached dangerous proportions before the glass began to rise once more, but the knowledge that only sailing ships follow this track across the southern ocean gives a feeling of isolation and increases the seriousness of any accident.

Towards evening, the sun broke through the flying clouds astern of us, and shining through the crests of the breaking waves turned them a translucent green, beneath the dazzling white tops, in indescribable beauty.

Our course had taken us about twenty miles north of the Auckland Islands but rain squalls had denied any possibility of sighting them. Then during the gale, to keep the wind right astern while dealing with refractory sails, the ship had been run so far off to the north east that the captain decided to pass between Bounty Island and the Antipodes Islands. Though none of these Islands scattered well to the southward of New Zealand is now permanently inhabited, attempts have been made in the past to settle them, and most of them were visited regularly until the fur seals were killed out by senseless butchery. Lack of regular communications more than anything else discourages their permanent exploitation, for even the southernmost, Macquarie Island, in $54\frac{1}{2}°$ S., has a climate no worse than that of the Falkland Islands except that perhaps a fine day may be less rare in the latter.

Where the full strength of the westerlies strike Macquarie Island, nothing but moss will grow, but in sheltered places ferns and tussock grass are abundant. Albatrosses, prions, terns, gulls, skuas, cormorants and duck breed there, as well as four species of penguins, sea elephants and sea leopards. Until a few years ago, a remarkable flightless parrot was peculiar to the island, but unhappily it was exterminated by cats, which were left there by sealers and have multiplied.

Sir Douglas Mawson has urged that Macquarie Island should be kept as a reserve for sub-antarctic fauna and flora and that the meteorological station should be re-established there, with perhaps a fur

44

[*facing:* Running before a gale in the Southern O●

seal farm to pay for its maintenance. He considers that a penguin egg industry might become an economic proposition. But as the island comes under the Government of Tasmania, it is doubtful whether anything can be done without Commonwealth assistance.

The Auckland Islands have three provision and clothing depots and a lifeboat on three of the Islands for the use of shipwrecked mariners. These are maintained by the New Zealand Government, which sends a ship to visit them once a year. Neither Bounty Island nor the Antipodes Islands was seen, for sailing ships prefer to keep well clear of the land, rarely sighting any from the time they leave Australia until the Cornish or Irish coast is made.

The actual navigation of sailing vessels and of steamships differs but little. The distance run is measured by a device called a patent log. A small propeller is towed behind the ship at the end of a long line. The rotation is conveyed by the line to counter gear on the stern of the ship, which shows on a small dial the actual mileage run through the water. Incidentally the propeller is sometimes bitten off by hungry sharks. The distance run, and the course steered, will together give a position, but obviously this will be influenced by wind and ocean currents, whose effect can only be estimated.

When out of sight of land the only method of finding out the ship's exact position is by taking observations for altitude of the sun, moon or stars. As the altitude is measured from the horizon, star sights can only be used at dawn and dusk during the short time that both the stars and horizon are visible. Though latitude can be found when a heavenly body is on the meridian, i.e., the north and south line overhead, to obtain longitude, it is necessary to know the exact time. This is given by the chronometer, which is an accurate clock, compensated so carefully that its daily error is small and quite regular. So important is time, that most ships carry two or three chronometers so that they can be used to check each other.

Time signals broadcast by wireless are now used to obtain the error of chronometers, while in the days before wireless when ships were in harbour, the dropping of a time ball or the firing of a gun fulfilled the same purpose.

A good story is told about the one o'clock gun which used to be fired at Hobart. It could be heard all over the town so that it became the general habit of everyone to pull out and check their watches as they heard the report. A leading but absent-minded citizen who had just acquired a set of false teeth came out of his office one day just as the gun fired. He was seen to stop, take out his teeth and look at them intently for a moment.

As sailing ships carry no wireless, or at least only a set capable of receiving the usual broadcast programmes within a limited range, complete reliance must be placed on the chronometers. But even the best ones in the world will not give a position if the heavens are clouded. As such conditions may persist for two or three weeks on end in the southern ocean, the accumulated errors of steering and patent log, added to the leeway and the effects of current, make the master of a sailing vessel give the land a reasonably wide berth.

On the seventeenth day we crossed the date line, as the one hundred and eightieth meridian is called, which gave our week eight days with two Fridays. Sailors will tell you that they have never heard of two Saturdays or two Sundays, nor could we find out if there was any precedent for two Good Fridays. In reckoning the length of the voyage the extra day is not included officially, for as the ship goes east the clocks are put on some twenty minutes daily, which will amount to about fourteen hours by the time England is reached.

Except for a few hours, ten days earlier, it was not until the twenty-third day that the ship first heeled over to starboard. It took some time to get accustomed to the new list and one could almost sympathize with old shellbacks who yarn about ships being on one tack for so long that barnacles began to grown on the lee side of their decks. Which way the ship listed made little difference unless it made it too easy to fall out of one's bunk.

Every day at noon the ship's clocks are corrected.

If the sun obliges there is almost a ceremony, for the captain watches the altitude of the sun through his sextant and the moment it begins to decrease he shouts 'eight glasses' in Swedish, when the helmsman strikes eight bells which is repeated on the big ship's bell on the forecastle. 'Eight glasses' has come down from the old days when half-hour sand glasses were used.

CHAPTER V

ON MEALS AND THE COOK

It is evening in the South Pacific. The shattering noise of a gong, beaten heavily within a few feet of us by the cheerful steward's boy, announces the triumphant production of another meal. In spite of the staggering of the ship and the slithering of the pots and pans on the big range, the cook never failed to make the best of the materials at his disposal and was always punctual to the minute, whatever the state of the weather.

In the galley the food is put into a basket and as the steward's boy has to run the gauntlet along the upper deck, dodging cold seas or spray for half the length of the ship, it is really remarkable if it arrives really hot. The dishes and cold plates are placed on a table near the door of the saloon, and after helping ourselves in turn there comes the difficulty of reaching one's seat at the other end of the compartment unbruised, and yet with food unspilt. When the ship is heeling over this is no mean feat, for when she lurches, even the matting underfoot is liable to slip on the varnished wood. The saloon is lit by hanging oil lamps which swing in a most disconcerting manner.

The captain comes in with a cheerful smile and

D

squeaking sea boots, clad in a furlined coat such as a trapper might wear. The rest of us are a motley collection bulging with everything possible in the way of winter woollies, high-necked sweaters and scarves, mostly of dingy colours. Two weary-eyed mates who have just come off a six-hour watch have on thick leather coats, and rubber thigh boots still glistening with wet. A ten-days'-old beard adds a touch of grimness to the scene, and the sound of the seas and of the wind whistling and moaning through the rigging makes the silence of the meal more marked. For whether it is the enormous appetites caused by the great cold or the desire to eat while the food is still warm, there is no conversation till the meal is nearly over. This is just as well as concentration on one's plate is necessary; often it must be held in the hand to prevent the contents from spilling. Wooden partitions, called fiddles, are fixed across the top of the tables to keep things from sliding. The tables themselves are fixed, but not the chairs, so that one leg must be coiled around a table leg or pushed against something immovable.

The cook in a sailing ship leads a difficult and depressing life. In cold weather the crew are invariably hungry, and it is the cook who is blamed whenever they feel they could eat any more. In the tropics he is expected to make salt horse appetizing. Each day of each week has its own fixed menu, which is the same whether it is hot or cold, except that lime-juice is served out in the tropics.

L'Avenir having been a training ship, the galley is large and has a preparing room next to it. When the ship is heeled over and lively, a too spacious galley is anything but a blessing for it gives the sensation of a beginner on skates setting out to cross a rink. If the damp sacking on the tiled floor once starts to slip, you are ruined.

It is during week-ends in cold weather that the cook gets most embittered, for then the lads bring along their carefully hoarded drop of water to warm it up for washing. The rings on top of the range get dragged out and left so that the next roll will slide them down between the stove and the bulkhead. Or suddenly there will be a hiss and a cloud of steam as a bucket capsizes its contents into the fire. Then will follow loud lamentations from the owner on the loss of his precious water, and even louder curses from the unsympathetic cook whose fire has been almost put out.

Cleanliness is a Scandinavian trait and the cook is no exception. Formerly no special cook was signed on for a sailing ship, but one of the crew was picked more or less at random for this duty, rarely keeping it for more than a few weeks. Nowadays the cook in a sailing ship hopes to become a steward as the latter gets higher wages than the chief mate.

The tea at meals is brought round on the whisky-and-soda principle. A finger of very strong tea is diluted with hot water. As fresh water is precious, this method ensures that very little is wasted. As in the old days, 'salt horse' appears regularly on the table. Actually it is beef which has been put into a cask of brine, bones and all, at Mariehamn. Difficult to cut, it is harder to bite. Old sailors really and honestly enjoy it, but judging from the comments of the youngsters on board, it must take years and years to reach this enviable state. However it is quite palatable when made up into a moist potato hash of ninety per cent potato. Twice a week there is thick pea-soup with cubes of salt pork, followed by a mountain of pancakes. There are potatoes at every meal; they keep their jackets on for breakfast. Twice a week the cook bakes excellent white and brown bread. 'Mousetrap Cheese' proved a good standby, especially at breakfast, and we were agreeably surprised by the great variety of excellent tinned things, both meat, fish and vegetables. A sort of thick soup made from dried fruits is a regular dish and probably a very healthy one.

But it was the killing of a pig that made a real treat as it provided chops, roast pork, liver pudding and blood pancakes. We never really appreciated the latter even when hot, but when one saw them eaten cold at breakfast smothered in red jam, they made desire fail utterly.

Of the private stores we brought, the fruit, nuts, biscuits and chocolate proved to be the most useful. We had been lucky in finding an excellent fruiterer in Port Pirie who supplied plums that kept for two months, oranges that lasted until the tropics, and lemons which were wrapped in paper and were still good at the end of the voyage. There is no need for cold storage in the South Pacific.

CHAPTER VI

THE CREW

As might be expected since they come from the Aaland Islands, the Swedish element predominates on board Captain Eriksson's ships, and Swedish is the language used. On board *L'Avenir* there were the following nationalities: Finns, Swedish Finns, Swedes, Germans, Danes, Belgians and three British (English, Canadian, and the Australian stowaway).

Nowadays, except for petty officers it is rare to find a full-grown man wanting to sign on a sailing ship. They are manned almost entirely by boys, ranging from fourteen to twenty years old, who come from good families, and hope to become officers in merchant ships. In most Scandinavian countries, two or three years' service in a sailing ship is compulsory before a candidate may sit for his mate's ticket.

Captain Gustaf Eriksson will not sign on any boy until he has made one round trip to Australia as an apprentice at a premium of fifty pounds. After completing this, he may sign on as an ordinary seaman at small wage for a second voyage, and as an able seaman at about two pounds a month for a third. *L'Avenir's* crew was made up of four able seamen, thirteen ordinary seaman and seven apprentices, none of whom had made more than two previous voyages. There are three petty officers; the sailmaker, who was a first-class seaman; the donkeyman, who did not profess to be one, and the carpenter, or 'timmerman' as he is in Swedish, which of course became 'timberman' to us.

The steward is responsible under the captain for the victualling of the whole ship: both he and the cook had a boy to fetch and carry for them.

After this voyage, *L'Avenir* will carry a smaller crew. The large number was only required because a great deal of work was necessary, when Captain Gustaf Eriksson bought her to get her into an efficient condition.

On one of the last days at Port Germein while in the one general store, we heard a fair-haired shock-headed boy ordering some cocoa and jam, and paying for it. Two days later, after we had sailed, happening to meet him aloft, we asked if it had arrived safely. His face fell as he told us it had not, adding: 'That comes under the heading of a national calamity, to come away without jam or cocoa'. All this was in perfect English. This was Dennis, a Finn whose parents had lived in England for many years, and who was educated at Taunton School. Although he had his twentieth birthday on board, this is the third sailing ship he has served in besides some time in a steamer. He was in the *Hougomont* when she was dismasted for the last time. On the conclusion of this voyage Dennis has got to do a year's military training, for being unable to speak Finnish he cannot carry out his service in the navy. He hopes to get into the cavalry, presumably because the horses understand Swedish.

The German boys in the crew are making their last voyage in *L'Avenir*, for recently Hitler has forbidden Germans to do their training in foreign ships. This order was not popular, for discipline is stricter in the German sailing ships and there is a lot of standing up and saluting to be done.

The reason for Hitler's edict is to check the present overcrowding in the German mercantile marine. Training in sail is compulsory for anyone wanting to become an officer, and though they are booked up for years ahead, the German training ships can keep a sufficient flow to meet the requirements of the present time.

'Adenoid Albert' is a native of Hamburg, talks quite good American, and is something of a know-all; he is tall, lanky and always hungry. One day after he had been working in a lifeboat, the mate took the precaution of inspecting its contents, when he found that Adenoid Albert had managed to abstract some of the emergency supply of biscuits. Adenoid Albert missed his next watch below.

On the voyage out there were some fowls on board. After a time these were noticed to lay unaccountably badly — until Adenoid Albert was discovered hidden

56

away somewhere, boiling a nice fresh egg over the stump of a candle.

The 'Kaiser's nephew' is a small polite lad who in cold weather wears a smart German military greatcoat. He does not actually claim to be a nephew but stoutly maintains that he is a relative of the Kaiser, to whom he occasionally writes. But, as the captain says, anyone can do that. Though he has been in sailing ships for nearly three years, this lad hates going aloft, so that when he developed symptoms of appendicitis just as a lot of chipping and painting of masts was to be done, the uncharitable ascribed it to loss of nerve.

Early in the voyage a slightly built boy with refined features, having just finished a trick at the wheel, came aft to the mate and reported the course he had been steering in perfect English. The mate said 'What's that?' sharply, when the course was repeated in Swedish.

This was Johnnie, the English apprentice.

He had felt the magic of the sea so strongly, that at three days' notice he had left his father's office and had quitted the straight, clear, if dull road, mapped out for him, in order to court adventure. Naturally his parents were not very pleased about it for he could only say that he hoped to be a Thames pilot, which seemed to be a feeble reason in support of a yardarm versus an office stool.

Johnie was well thought of by the captain and mates although he was completely ignorant of seamanship and navigation when first he came on board. He is now given his fair share of seaman's jobs aloft. On the voyage out to Australia he learnt to speak Swedish well, which accounted for the mate's attitude as just quoted. He is generally liked, but the crew and the other apprentices cannot get over the fact that besides being inclined to keep to himself, Johnie reads Milton. To be fair one must state that his enjoyment of literature is not confined to Milton, whose verse he learnt to appreciate from lack of other books. He is also something of an artist and was much in demand for drawing sketches of sailing ships on sharks' fins and for painting designs on models.

George, the stowaway, was born at Broken Hill, the great mining district of New South Wales. He has tried his hand as a blacksmith and as a carpenter, spending four years wandering round Victoria, New South Wales, and South Australia looking for work, after having quarrelled with his stepfather.

He had often thought of going to sea, but it was only when staying with friends at Port Pirie and when he heard that there were three sailing ships at Port Germein, that the way seemed clear. Though of course he would not breathe a word about it, it was almost certain that some of the crew knew he was hiding on board before the ship sailed, but saw no reason to mention it. George admitted that someone passed within three feet of him while he was on the prowl one night. The sailmaker, who has his meals in his cabin, had also noticed that some butter had disappeared, but ascribed it to cats or rats.

Referring to his first interview with the captain, George said: 'He was very angry. He was shaking almost as much as I was'. For a time he must have felt like a criminal but it was not long before he proved himself such a hard worker and so invariably cheerful under the most impossible conditions that soon he was regarded as an ordinary member of the crew. Though he had been given various articles of clothing he always seemed to be wet, underclad, and cold in bad weather, but was never the smallest bit cast down.

George was not popular with the third mate or the cook. The former disapproved of his swearing in English, and the latter did not appreciate his ideas of humour. When it was George's turn to draw the salthorse for the forecastle from the galley, he would come in as if he owned the place and say breezily, 'To-day, I'll have a nice piece of steak, some cauliflower and roast potatoes'. When told off to fetch coal from the bunker to the locker in the galley he would begin by bringing buckets of dust; when the cook objected, he would attempt to bargain with him, suggesting a couple of cakes for each bucket of knobs.

Of course, though he had never done so in his life

before, George had to go aloft at once. He acquitted himself well but admitted that he did not like looking down for the first few days. It is always much easier aloft if one is not alone. Imagination does not have such a free hand, and fear is swamped by all sorts of other feelings, such as the desire to show off.

Towards the end of the voyage George suddenly announced his intention of making a model. The sailmaker seemed to be doing most of the work, having most deftly shaped the hull with a razor-sharp axe, but when this was suggested, George said: 'Well anyhow I scrounged the lump of wood'.

His plans for the future were naturally very vague for he did not know whether he would be handed over to the police on arrival, or, if not, whether he would be allowed to land. Though he had a friend in England, he was not at all sure of his whereabouts. He would often ask if we thought there was any possibility of his being allowed to join the navy in spite of having no papers.

Jackie was the girl apprentice, but she was called 'Yackie' by the Scandinavians.

Here was no striving after the limelight but a most amazingly genuine passion for the sea. Still in her early twenties, she had spent most of her life in Montreal, reading and studying everything that has been written about ships, and even taking a correspondence course in navigation. To gain practical

top: The captain and the mate vainly looking for the sun in the Southern Ocean. Heavy seas coming up from astern

bottom: The watch working on a yard. Jackie is the second figure from the right

knowledge of the details of rigging, she made a model of a clipper ship which took three years to complete.

While in England, she attended a navigation school in Limehouse for a time, but found this disappointing as the teaching was more about the examiners than navigation. The instructor would warn the class: 'If Captain Smith asks you, you must say this, but if it is Captain Jones, you must say that, though of course in practice you would do it quite differently.'

Captain Gustaf Eriksson was the only ship-owner Jackie could find who would take her as an apprentice, and she said 'being a dame' she had to pay twice as much as the other apprentices. But she did have the definite amenity of a cabin aft and meals with the captain and mates. As for ship's work, she did exactly the same as any other member of the crew, going aloft, chipping, painting, and taking her trick at the wheel, except when it was blowing hard.

The captain takes his duties as chaperon most seriously, and when she came on board, he made her promise not to fall in love with any of the crew.

She has a most cheerful laugh and one would expect her to be very popular. But besides the superstition which puts head winds and calms to her account, there is no doubt that the crew do resent her presence on board. It is hard to get at the real reason. Probably it has something to do with the belittling of their hardships. The cheap newspapers write up a good story about her, saying that she does everything, and is treated exactly the same as the rest of the crew, who doubtless get taunted with leading a girl's life. In actual fact, though it is in no way her fault, Jackie has a much easier existence than the crew. Besides a dry cabin and better food served nicely, the mates inevitably give her a certain amount of consideration. Against this must be set loneliness. She cannot go into the forecastle, and in cold weather there is no other common ground for meeting apprentices and boys off watch. It would obviously be unsuitable if she were to spend too much time aft and become too friendly with the mates.

The problem is a difficult one, but the experience of a voyage convinced one that the sea is a hopeless profession for a girl to adopt, however enthusiastic she may be.

The crew is split up into two equal watches which are picked at the beginning of the voyage, the chief mate having the port and the second mate the starboard watch.

At sea the twenty-four hours is split up into the following periods:

PORT WATCH	STARBOARD WATCH
Midnight to 4 a.m.	4 a.m. to 8 a.m.
8 a.m. to 1 p.m.	1 p.m. to 7 p.m.
7 p.m. to midnight	Midnight to 4 a.m.
4 a.m. to 8 a.m.	

and so on throughout the voyage.

When not required for working the ship, the watch on deck is employed in chipping, painting, refitting work, etc., from 6 a.m. to 6 p.m., after which they must be ready to come up at a moment's notice at the sound of two blasts on a whistle which is carried by the mate on watch. The watch on deck must provide a helmsman, a 'policeman', who is responsible for rousing out the hands when required and is always available for odd jobs, and also a lookout on the forecastle-head at night. At night in the tropics when nearly all the crew sleep on deck, if two whistles are blown, both watches usually turn out as they probably do not know whose watch it should be.

The watch on deck is sufficient for bracing round the yards, but for shortening sail the watch below is often used as well, unless there is no hurry.

Certain 'daymen' do not belong to a watch but work from 6 a.m. to 5 p.m., with half an hour for breakfast, an hour for dinner, and half an hour for coffee at 3.30 p.m. Normally these are the sailmaker, the carpenter and the donkeyman, but according to the size of the crew, the latitude, and the amount of work to be done, extra hands may be taken out of watches and put on day work. In *L'Avenir*, the sailmaker had two mates almost continuously. Except in bad weather, the crew get an adequate amount of sleep, provided they can take it at odd times; but the two mates, who have to keep every minute of their watch on deck, and whose mealtime comes from their watch below, must find these long voyages very wearing.

Though most ships carry a third mate, he always keeps watch under the chief mate, getting most of the unpleasant odd jobs of the ship.

CHAPTER VII

CALM

HAVING made a succession of good days' runs, someone rashly predicted that we should be round the Horn in ten days. Almost immediately the wind began to ease, which was the prelude to a long calm. Gradually the swell disappeared and often with eyes closed, it was easier to imagine oneself in a refrigerator on land, than in a ship at sea two thousand miles from anywhere; for while reflecting on our predicament, we found that we were near that point on the globe which is farthest from land in any direction.

And yet by some freak of fancy the skyline took on an oddly friendly and reassuring appearance as if something familiar was only just over the horizon.

On the thirtieth day in about 49° S. and 132° W. we were near a spot marked on the chart with a sounding of 2467 fathoms, about 2·8 land miles. According to Sir John Murray, if a successful trawling of the sea floor in this area is made, the net will contain several hundreds of shark's teeth and dozens of ear bones of whales. Some of these will belong to extinct species.

Doctor Johnson once remarked that no man will be a sailor who has contrivance enough to get himself into a jail; also that when men come to like a sea life, they are not fit to live on land.

Of the variety of excellent excuses or justifications for being a sailor, perhaps the strongest and most logical is simply that there is such a quantity of sea. Over two-thirds (seventy-one per cent, to be more exact) of the surface of the globe is water. But what is to many people more appalling still is that the average depth of oceans and seas is two and a quarter miles. Land is being washed into the sea by rain, rivers and waves with such rapidity that after six million years there will be none left. Long-sighted parents will therefore look to the sea for a sure employment for their sons.

Though huge areas of the sea bottom are still unexplored, it is generally more featureless than land and with much gentler slopes. The greatest depth found up to the present is about six and a quarter miles; this is in the Pacific off the Phillipine Islands. Light only penetrates down between half a mile and a mile, but in all this layer vegetable life is present in the form of vast floating meadows.

In the Abyssal Zones are absolute darkness, an unchanging temperature slightly above the freezing point of fresh water and an enormous pressure, which at three miles down amounts to about three tons per square inch. There is no live vegetation and the sea floor is covered with a soft ooze.

Life exists throughout the whole mass of the oceans

down to the greatest depth, where some creatures eat the mud with the particles of dead vegetable matter which have rained down from above. These are preyed upon by frightful looking carnivorous animals with enormous mouths and wicked teeth. Deep sea fish have either huge over-developed eyes or else are blind.

The barometer rose depressingly slowly and steadily each day until it was higher than that recorded in the ship's logs for the previous two years. Ship noises almost ceased except for the hollow thuds of chipping hammers wielded by the watch on deck from 6 a.m. to 6 p.m. They were working in the cable lockers and in the after store-room, and, descending with candles, the boys looked like miners going down to the pits.

Conrad says, 'the true peace of God begins at any spot a thousand miles from the nearest land'. Virtually we were in retreat, and things of the outside world had dropped away. There was no trace of boredom, but the smallest incident on board assumed great importance and interested everybody.

Conveniently on a Sunday immediately after the midday meal when everyone was free, a huge whale spent an hour cruising about under the bowsprit. Deep down it was just a shape, but as it rose slowly a glistening dark grey mound broke the surface and there was a hissing and sighing sound as it exhaled from its double blowhole. When it dived submarine fashion the huge horizontal flukes of its tail could be seen clearly, and for some distance one could follow the succession of swirls left by each stroke. As the whale was at least fifty feet long and was obviously at a loose end, it seemed a wicked waste of energy which might well have been used to tow us out of this in-infernal calm. It was of the blue species, which grows to eighty-five feet or more in length; such a monster would weigh over three hundred tons, but as it could not swallow even a very little Jonah, its tonnage by Thames measurement must be negligible.

During the course of one night, Josephina the cat had annoyed everyone by leaping on to their bunks, and had been chased out of each cabin in turn. It should be explained that when the ship is deep loaded, the portholes must be kept permanently closed, and so cabin doors are usually left open for ventilation. The mates had had their short sleep broken by the cat, and had ejected her with cursings. But the second mate had to go on watch at midnight; this gave Josephina her opportunity and by the time he came down, she was sitting proudly on his bunk with a family of three.

The killing of a pig featured for us in enormous headlines as does a popular murder to the general public. Two of the crew carried out the condemned animal to the well-deck, where a grating had been rigged up on boxes like a Druid's altar. Happily this had no special meaning for the pig, who was wondering in terms of food what this change of surroundings might mean. Then came the steward with a bucket and brush to carry out some preliminary washing, followed by the executioner with hammer and knife, and the chef in full regalia and with a basin. There was a respectful hush among the spectators broken by the dull whack of the hammer, and then in a moment the chef was rapidly stirring the basin so that the much-looked-forward-to blood pudding should reach expectations. Frassie, the captain's tabby cat, watched the whole operation with ghoulish interest, for pig is his obsession, and when it has been hung up he keeps a permanent watch beneath each corpse for fragments shaken down by accident or friend.

We had sailed from Australia with eight live pigs on board and while buying them near Port Germein, the captain had had an amusing incident, for while they were in the farmyard, the farmer proclaimed with a proud air: 'Now there's a *beautiful* pig.' After looking at it closely for a moment, all the captain said was: 'Yes, but it's dead.' And so it was.

The next Sunday night, a considerable disturbance was caused when one of the crew suddenly began to chase the sailmaker all over the ship, cursing him and yelling loud threats to kill him. At first it was thought to be a case of madness. Luckily the second mate, being a powerful man, was able to deal with the situation by chucking him into a cabin and locking him in. But as the yells continued and the door did not seem too secure, the sailmaker was given sanctuary aft, though even there he passed a somewhat anxious night.

Eventually it came to light that two of the crew, having got hold of some bottles of rum, had been enjoying a private carouse, and that the particular one who had given trouble invariably wanted to commit murder when drunk. One of the boys showed a four-inch scar on the back of his head where this savage had hit him with a bottle.

The calm lasted for nine days, or at least during that time we made an average of just over 1° a day to the eastward instead of the normal 5°, though sometimes we went quite a long way in other directions. Though we felt sure the calm covered a large area and would probably affect all the ships which had left the Spencer Gulf within a few days of us, it killed all hope of winning the grain race, or even of making a reasonably fast passage. Calms just before, between, and immediately after the Trades are to be expected, and it is rarely that ships get past any of them without some delay, but nine days lost in the Southern Ocean, where westerly gales should blow permanently, is time lost irretrievably. There have been very long passages to Cape Horn. The *Herzogin Cecilie*, winner of several races, once took seventy days to round it from Australia. But this was because on leaving the Spencer Gulf, meeting with easterly winds, it was decided to make for the Cape of Good Hope. When well on the way, the easterly winds petered out and were succeeded by such convincing westerlies that she was forced to go round the Horn after all.

Apart from being the most southerly point on the ship's track, after which she turns to the north and home, Cape Horn fills everyone's horizon as does the actual mountain peak to a party of climbers. Once it has been achieved, though the dangers and hardships are not yet over, all thoughts are directed towards a successful end.

Therefore the days lost during the calm seemed to be sheer waste, and the time seemed to pass slowly, for, as there was no heating system of any sort on board, it was so bitterly cold between decks that reading was impossible, except for a few minutes at a time. There was a large track chart pinned up outside the pantry, with the ship's position marked on it, and often one would notice people working out roughly the number of days after Cape Horn before warmer weather could be expected.

CHAPTER VIII

ALBATROSSES, PETRELS AND PRIONS

IT would be impossible to conceive a more dreary existence than that of the sea-birds of the Southern Ocean. Even the life of a sailor is nothing like as homeless or restless. Many of these birds spend most of their life out of sight of land, soaring and wheeling ceaselessly over the stormy seas, except for the few months of the breeding season when they find some remote rocky island in the far south, where they congregate.

Albatrosses and petrels can at least consider themselves fortunate in laying only one egg at a time, as the young bird has to be fed for many weeks, until it becomes so immensely fat that it can go on living in the nest after the parent birds have left, and until it can fly.

Presumably sleep is unnecessary for these birds of the open ocean, unless perhaps they can take it by the minute as they glide down towards the water from a height.

In a gale it would be quite impossible for them to remain on the sea to rest without constant vigilance to avoid breaking waves, while in calm weather one would imagine that they would always fear enemies from below.

Some days there are disappointingly few birds to be seen until a bucket of refuse is thrown over the side, when in the space of a few minutes a large patch of water will be covered with truculent wrangling birds. It is impossible to tell exactly what they will eat, but one thing is certain, that lemon or orange peel does not cause more than a second's hopeful interest. The larger albatrosses and petrels are rarely seen to settle

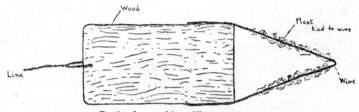

Device for catching Albatrosses

on the water by day to feed excepting on stuff thrown overboard. Their main diet is said to be cuttle-fish and small marine creatures, which come to the surface during the night.

Though albatrosses are generally supposed to be stupid birds, they are not by any means easy to catch if the ship has any way on, as any movement of the bait through the water arouses their suspicions. In order to deceive one, plenty of slack line should be kept in hand and when the quarry wheels towards the bait the line should be paid out quickly so that there is no drag. A piece of wire bent into a V with legs secured to a lump of wood can be used as a hook, salt horse being tied to the wire. The hooked beak of the albatross gets jammed in the V and as long as the strain is kept on the line it cannot be released. The line should be stout, for if the ship is moving ahead the hooked albatross may become partially submerged, and with its wings flapping on the surface will put a heavy strain on the gear. This happened with our first catch, but he was landed safely though slightly water-logged. He was a young Wandering Albatross and even on deck he was a magnificent sight, for his body was about the size of a swan's, and he had a wing spread of over ten feet, which is two feet short of the known maximum. As his legs would only support him for a moment or two, he sat quite peacefully until anyone approached too near, when he would make a quick and savage lunge. He made no sound except a hollow rattle as he closed or shook his huge hooked bcak.

Albatrosses are said to show symptoms of sea sickness when on board a ship, but ours was better mannered. They cannot fly off a ship's deck and this one did not even make an attempt. After being well photo-graphed, he was dropped off the stern, landing flat on the water with a resounding smack, in spite of having his wings spread. After being caught, albatrosses usually swim about for an hour or so; but this one made a short trial flight of some ten yards before settling down again. Some of the crew said they had

The second Mate holding the albatross, with Charlie, the steward's boy, looking on

seen the same bird caught again, immediately after it had been released.

The large family of petrels, which range in size from goose to starling, are supposed to have derived their name from St. Peter and his attempt to walk on the waters of the Sea of Galilee, for when feeding, they often remain on the wing hovering, touching the water with one foot or with both feet alternately. Some of them glide about like albatrosses though less perfectly, as they have to beat their wings more often, probably because they usually keep close to the water. The various species of petrels fly under many odd names, most of them given by sailors, such as Nelly, Cape hen, shearwater, Cape pigeon, Cape dove, fulmar, mutton-bird, hag, ice-bird, and whale-bird.

Except during the breeding season, though petrels spend all their time at sea, some will remain in an area more or less near where they have nested, while others migrate across the equator in the same purposeful way as land birds. By some mysterious means they find their way back to the breeding island, which is usually such a desolate comfortless spot, that one is inclined to think that it cannot matter much to them whether they reach the right one or not.

Most of the species nest in holes, which they excavate in soft ground, or else under stones or roots. The same species may use holes in one locality and stones in another. Some nest on ledges on cliffs or in the open; these can walk, whereas the legs of the burrowers are too weak to support them, so that on land they have to flap themselves along on their breasts.

Plumage varies from all black to all white, with over fifty combinations for adult birds; identification is therefore extremely difficult.

Prions, known to seamen as ice-birds or whale-birds, are small creatures which usually appear in flocks. They have white breasts and grey backs, which so tone with the sea that they seem to disappear when their breasts are turned away from one.

Storm petrels are the tiniest of the sea birds, and as they skim in and out between the hollows of the waves they remind one of swallows or martins. Sailors call them Mother Carey's chickens, Mother Carey being a corruption of Mater Cara, the Blessed Virgin Mary. So frail looking are these birds that one is filled with wonder that they can keep the sea, or rather the air, for months on end. During a storm, they feed in the wave valleys, dodging the seas skilfully as the crests curl over and break. They are sociable little creatures and usually when they do come, it is in fair numbers.

The old superstition that they foretell a storm can hardly have much foundation, as they were with us during the SE. trades, only deserting us for a short time when we were several degrees north of the equator and then returning for the rest of the voyage. Bad weather certainly brings a large flock to feed in the ship's wake, presumably on the minute creatures which are brought eddying up to the surface. Another reason may be that the wake of a ship provides an area of relatively calm water in which they can feed more comfortably.

The sense of companionship which all these birds of the ocean give is felt by everyone on board, and one never tired of watching the graceful beauty of their movements in the air.

CHAPTER IX

CAPE HORN AND TIERRA DEL FUEGO

In our restricted world, anything out of the ordinary causes amazing excitement and interest. On the forty-second day out, when still two days from the Horn, a sailing ship was sighted hull-down right astern. With yards squared to a following wind, her sails had a strangely solid appearance, probably because the distance was too great for the gaps between them to be seen.

In a moment everyone not on watch was on deck, looking at her, and the rest of the day was devoted to conjecturing who she might be. One thing was depressingly obvious to all — that she was sailing much faster than *L'Avenir*. During the afternoon she came up on our quarter, well to the southward, and we made her out to be a four-masted barque with double spanker gaffs. Expert opinion considered it might be the *Pamir* which had been loading in Sydney, the first big sailing vessel to go there for many years, and the first ship to have to house her topgallant masts to get under the Sydney Harbour Bridge. Neither the captain nor mates had ever before sighted another sailing ship in the vicinity of Cape Horn.

The cold was becoming even more intense, and except when it was very clear by day, a lookout was constantly stationed on the forecastle to watch for ice. As a rule the icebergs in the southern ocean are not more than about half a mile long. They come from the ice barrier which surrounds the Antarctic continent, the edges of which break off in summer, and go floating off to the northward. Even at night these large icebergs can usually be seen by the iceblink, which is a sort of halo, appearing over them. Quite small icebergs are really more dangerous to ships, for they are hard to see and yet may be large enough to rip out the side plating of a fast-moving ship. When the proximity of ice is suspected, careful sea and air temperatures are taken at frequent intervals. It is essential to pass to windward of an iceberg as all the bits that break off the parent are drifted away to leeward.

A phenomenally big iceberg was sighted at the end of 1854 and it remained an awful danger to ships for five months, during which it travelled from 44° S. 28° W. to 40° S. 20° W. In one place this huge iceberg was 300 feet high, but the main danger was that it was shaped like a hook with the shank sixty miles long and with the bend forming a bay forty miles across. An emigrant ship, the *Guiding Star*, was embayed and lost with all hands, while two other ships were only extricated by the fine seamanship of their captains. In the South Atlantic ice sometimes gets as far up as 36° S.

The following morning we had reached the area marked in large letters on the chart 'storms and almost constant rain prevail here'. The glass was falling, the wind was freshening and there was a bleak misty rain which precluded any possibility of sighting the other barque.

By evening it was blowing a gale, and the ship was tearing along in a welter of foam with the well-deck constantly full of water. At 8 p.m. the royals were furled. Shortly afterwards there was a crash on deck. The weather main lower topgallant brace had parted and the block had fallen down, mercifully without hitting anybody. The wind continued to freshen and, as seas were coming over the upper deck with increasing frequency and determination, a further mark of respect was paid to Cape Horn by furling all the topgallants and the mizen upper topsail.

Everyone working on deck was wet through, for seaboots became cisterns, and if one has to move about it is impossible to prevent the sea from finding its way down between neck and oilskin collar. But things might well have been worse. For if our upper deck had not been almost continuous, nearly all the work would have been done waist deep in water. The temperature had risen, and was slightly higher than usual off the Horn. One year late in the season, the *Winterhude* had a bad time in this region. The spray coming on board froze all the ropes on deck, so that none of the braces could be used, nor could the sails have been clewed up. Luckily the gale held steady and remained moderate or she must have been in very grave danger.

Both watches spent most of the night on the spray-swept deck or else aloft in the full force of the biting wind, but yet everyone was keyed up by the knowledge that we really were passing quickly through these dreaded waters, and that the crux of the voyage was near. Towards morning the wind eased enough for the captain to leave the deck, and a few hours later the ship, though shortened down, had got back into normal routine. At 6 a.m. chipping began as usual, and one had the feeling that at least those doing it were in shelter. We found that during the night a heavy sea had come over the weather side into the well-deck and, being deflected up by the bulkhead of the donkey boiler house, had lifted the spare royal yard from its securings and had bent the iron rails above it.

We were now sixty to one hundred miles south of Cape Horn, which is rarely sighted by sailing ships for several excellent reasons. Fifty-six miles south-west of the Horn there is a formidable group of rocky islands — Diego Ramirez — which spread over six miles in length. We had had no sights for several days and the strength of the current which flows towards the Atlantic varies from five to forty miles a day. The compass itself has errors which can be found and allowed for, but even a perfect helmsman cannot keep exactly to his course in a heavy sea. Each wave will throw the ship off one way or the other, and though the wheel is put over at once to counteract this, it takes a little time for the helm to take effect, so that the ship's track presents a distinctly wavy appearance to the albatross's eye. The mean result is closer to the course desired according to the skill of the helmsman in anticipating each yaw. Needless to add there are no useful lighthouses anywhere near Cape Horn. No ships except the few remaining barques use this old road, and in these days lighthouses are not erected for their benefit.

Though the ship was a long way from shore we did have one link with it in the form of a small brown land-bird which settled for a moment in the weather shrouds. Then it was blown away to leeward, to continue struggling against the wind till its strength failed. We wished it could have understood that it had reached safety, and that on board it would have been looked after as an honoured visitor, at least until arrival at Falmouth. There perhaps the customs officials might have put a seal upon its cage lest it might be the bearer of some Patagonian plague. For, since the parrot disease introduced a few years ago, any visiting caged bird, however respectable looking it may be, is treated as a suspicious character. Perhaps, after all, the bird may have chosen the better end, keeping its freedom, and going on hoping to sight land until it fell exhausted. It is rare that landbirds live for long

on board ship, for they do not seem to care for salt
horse or wheat, and are liable to grow steadily weaker
until somehow the cat manages to get hold of them.

The island of Tierra del Fuego, the 'Land of Fire',
was so named by Magellan during the first night he

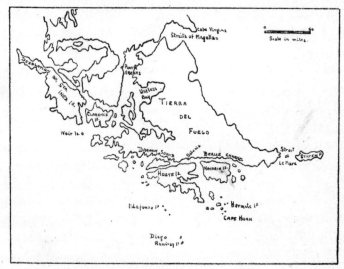

Tierra del Fuego and Cape Horn

approached it in the year 1520, because of the many
fires which were sighted on its shores.

The danger of the coast, and of the natives that
frequent it, is so notorious that we read all there was
on board on the subject, in case of possible shipwreck.
The following extracts from an old edition of Findlay's
Directory of the South Pacific Ocean are of interest, as they

help one to realize the anxieties which must have filled the mind of the mariner some fifty years ago.

'The natives are low in stature, their colour is a dirty copper or dark mahogany and their only clothing is a seal or dear skin worn with the hair outwards. They are thievish and greedy . . . caution should be used in dealing with them especially in vessels weakly manned.

'There is nothing of the graceful gliding of the North American or of the New Zealand canoe in their miserable boats. Instead of being propelled by paddles, they are rowed by oars rudely made from pieces of board tied on to the end of a pole. The canoes also instead of being hollowed out from the trunk of a large tree into a pretty shape, or made of bark like those of Canada, are simply planks tied together with fibres without the slightest regard to form. On the bottom in the middle is a small fire and on each side will be found six or eight men, women, and children according to the size of the boat. They are generally almost naked, the women appearing to care less about clothing than the men, though either will sell you any skin they have on for a little biscuit or tobacco.

'Admiral Fitzroy, on his first voyage in 1830, brought two boys and a girl from the South Coast to England where they were most kindly treated and educated for three years; showing much aptness and leading to great hopes that they might be the means of ameliorating the condition of their countrymen. But within a few weeks of their restoration to their native haunts, on his second voyage, they had relapsed into their primitive barbarism. However, the impressions made were permanent, for in 1853 Captain Parker Snow met with one of them, Jimmy Button, then a wild, naked, shaggy-looking savage, who still retained his knowledge of English and had imparted it to his relatives, but who was unmistakably the dangerous creature that his untutored brethren were. The noble kindness and sympathy shown by Admiral Fitzroy to these outcasts has been unfortunately of little avail; and the subsequent well intended but misguided efforts of the Patagonian Mission have also failed in lessening the barbarism of these people. Indeed, they are now much more to be dreaded than at any earlier period, for they have attacked and overcome the crews of vessels passing through these channels.'

Punta Arenas, in the Straits of Magellan, is the only considerable town in a large area, 'the exports being wool and skins, gold, sealskins, ostrich feathers and lumber'. There are coal mines in the vicinity but these are now abandoned.

Ushuaia being in 54° 49 minutes S. is the southernmost white settlement on the globe, having originally been founded by missionaries in 1867. It is now the headquarters of the Argentine officials in Tierra del

Fuego, and a depot is maintained there for the relief of shipwrecked mariners.

'Spaniard Harbour possesses a very melancholy interest, as it was here that a party of zealous missionaries headed by Captain Alan F. Gardiner and R. Williams, Surgeon, seven in number, perished most miserably of starvation between June and September 1851.'

'The Cape Horn group of Islands rise to mountain peaks one thousand to two thousand feet high, and are thickly wooded to their summits. For six years there was a mission station on one of the islands, but the inclement weather caused it to be given up.'

There has arisen a tradition of tragedy about Cape Horn, for the outlying rocks and the awful weather have together exacted a heavy toll of life. There have been few survivors from those ships which have come to grief. Disasters were of course much more frequent in the days when ships used to beat round from the eastward, for often when they thought that they had got well to the westward of Cape Horn and that it was safe to make to the north, adverse currents had so impeded their progress that suddenly through the darkness or driving rain rocks would be seen to leeward. Usually it would be blowing too hard to tack, so that it would be necessary to wear, i.e. go about stern to wind. If the visibility was poor, there might be insufficient room, when the ship and her people would be doomed unless she could thread a way through the rocks to regain the open sea.

It is years since sailing ships have needed to round the Horn against the westerlies, as there are now no cargoes offered from South American ports. But no doubt Cape Horn is biding its time.

CHAPTER X

MORE CALM

PART of the fascination of the sea lies in its unexpected changes and the strong contrasts it presents. For the first part of the voyage our horizon had been bounded by Cape Horn, and we felt as if we were attempting some difficult pass through a range of mountains. But though the Horn was passed, and the strain relaxed, we did not expect any immediate relief from cold westerly winds.

However on the forty-sixth day when about two hundred miles south of the Falkland Islands we were awakened by glorious sunshine streaming in through the porthole. The ship was just moving before a light breeze, which was barely enough to make the patent log revolve. Gradually the south-westerly swell decreased, and as the sun gained power, it was possible to enjoy being on deck.

As had often been observed in the early morning, very few seabirds were to be seen; but as the day went on, more collected about us, or could be sighted in the distance. This fact has been used to argue that the same albatrosses and petrels do not necessarily follow a ship for weeks on end, but that as each day breaks, her presence attracts such birds as happen to be in her vicinity. In calm weather albatrosses have to beat their wings fairly often, but when there is a swell, they appear to make use of the air currents caused by each wave, gathering speed while soaring along the trough and then gliding up as high as they can.

We were close to the scene of the Battle of the Falkland Islands, perhaps actually above the battered hull of one of the German cruisers *Scharnhorst* or *Gneisenau* which were sunk with most of their crews at the end of 1914. A remarkable incident occurred during the battle after the *Gneisenau* had been hit four times by heavy shell and had some fifty killed and wounded. To quote from John Irving's account: 'Now as though to bring a breath of peace and tranquillity to a scene of blood, a full-rigged ship was observed to pass down between the lines with her sails full and bellying with the slight breeze. What she was doing there no man knew, but more than one old seaman, with memories of Drake's drum, vowed that she could be no real ship but a phantom. She might well have been a visitor from the realms of the navy's glorious past laden with a precious cargo of tradition — Nelson, Hood, Howe, Drake, Grenville and a score more — all come to look on while fresh laurels were added to their navy's honour, and their comrade Craddock amply avenged.' History does not relate the name or nationality of this vessel, but we could easily imagine the thrill of hearing the distant boom of heavy gun fire, the sighting first, of columns of smoke, and then the masts, funnels and hulls as they came over the horizon, with the drab grey of their outlines being broken by the orange flashes of cordite. As they approached one would see the enormous spouts of water made by falling shell, and occasionally a sheet of flame as one found its mark. All eyes would be straining to make out flags or silhouettes, when there would come either exaltation or else a desperate and impotent despair as it was recognized which were friends and which foes. These thoughts made us wonder if there had been any threat to the peace of the world during the six weeks which had passed without news.

It was a common belief among old-fashioned sailors that ships and bodies would only sink to a depth where the pressure counteracted their weight. That they would 'find their level' and there float for evermore. Actually everything heavy sinks to the bottom, and without losing its outward appearance, except that hollow objects are eventually exploded inwards, or 'imploded', when the pressure overcomes the strength of the material of which they are made. Human and animal bodies are formed of such porous tissue that they reach great depths without showing external sign of change. When a ship sinks, all closed water-tight tanks or compartments are 'imploded', and the corks of any bottles not quite full are forced in. Otherwise she remains the same in appearance.

The forty-seventh day was even more unique for the vicinity we were in, for there was hardly a breath of wind all day, and until afternoon the sky was cloudless. It was Conception Day, and therefore a holiday, so that everyone was able to spend the day on deck, revelling in the sunshine after the long weeks of bitter cold. An extraordinary stillness prevailed.

The day closed suitably with a glorious sunset. Without even the faintest breeze, the shining waters were gold towards the west and pink towards the east, while the swell caused ever-changing dark patterns to shadow the surface of the sea. Overhead the steely sky was cloudless, but above the horizon were banks of leaden mist with one delicate pink cloud flung over them like drapery of gauze. The reflection of the moon made a shimmering, wavy pathway over the sea. If sunsets in the far south are often as lovely as this, no wonder the Antarctic has such a fascination for explorers, who, in spite of unbelievable discomforts, are drawn back again and again. Unhappily beautiful sunsets in these waters do not appear to promise fair weather. Anson's chaplain in the *Centurion* wrote: 'We here found what was constantly verified by all our observations in these high latitudes, that fair weather was always of an exceeding short duration, and that when it was remarkably fine, it was a certain presage of a succeeding storm, for the calm and sunshine of our afternoon ended in a most turbulent night'. We were spared the storm, but after a night with the mercury only a few degrees above freezing, came a day of wretched drizzle with a moderate breeze heading us and a long swell coming from the eastward.

There is nothing better than a chart to set one's mind on to fresh or half-forgotten tracks. Noticing the name Elephant Island recalled one of the very finest boat journeys ever made. After the *Endurance* had been crushed in the ice and had sunk, Shackleton brought his crew over the ice with two small boats until at length they reached open water and Elephant Island, which is in 61°S. and some three hundred miles south of our track. The boats were far too small and crazy to contain all the party in safety, and as Shackleton considered that there was no hope of any rescue party finding them, he decided that however hazardous the project might be, he must go for help.

Though the Falkland Islands were less than six hundred miles away Shackleton knew that the prevailing westerly gales would prevent any boat from getting there, so he decided to run with the westerlies to South Georgia Island eight hundred miles away to leeward. The *James Caird*, the larger of their boats, was only twenty feet long, double-ended like a whaler, but weather-beaten and strained. Shackleton remarked 'she appeared to have shrunk in some mysterious way when I viewed her in the light of our new undertaking'. Normally she was quite open except in the bows, but with sledge runners and canvas, a deck was put over to keep out some of the spray. From the many volunteers Shackleton chose five, leaving Frank Wilde in command of the remainder of the crew.

With difficulty the boat was launched, loaded up with provisions, and navigated through the fringe of pack-ice. They steered to the northward for a couple of days to avoid the danger of ice, and in the hope of getting warmer weather. The expected westerly gales were encountered and for two days it was necessary to heave-to. Ice formed wherever the spray fell, so that the buoyancy of the boat was dangerously reduced. On the tenth day a huge wave nearly ended their voyage but by a miracle they survived and baled out the boat. Then came another anxiety. If the weather was continuously cloudy or their navigation was not exact they might easily overrun South Georgia, and being once to leeward, their boat would never be capable of beating back. Worsley was the navigator, but besides this, H. R. Mill says that it was his spirits that helped to 'uphold the men whose minds had not been trained to dominate the depressing drag of their racked and weary bodies'.

After fourteen days South Georgia was sighted, but their troubles were not yet over for their last cask of water was found slightly salt, and a strong gale forced them to heave-to again. It was two more days before they landed on the uninhabited side of this unmapped island. Though they all landed in safety two of the men were too ill to move, so that Shackleton and two companions made the first crossing of the island over mountains and glaciers ending up by going down a waterfall on the end of some alpine rope.

It was four months before Shackleton could reach South America and there, after several abortive attempts, organize a relief expedition; but the Elephant Island party were found well and in good spirits thanks to the leadership of Frank Wilde and their complete confidence in Shackleton.

As we passed over a hundred miles to the east of the Falkland Islands, we had to content ourselves with second-hand information about them, extracted from books.

The Admiralty Sailing Directions have much in common with Baedeker's Guides for mountainous countries, which usually make the very most out of all difficulties, cautioning the traveller against this peak or that 'which should only be hazarded by robust and steady-headed alpinists'.

But though the Sailing Directions give the mariner little hope of avoiding disaster for long, they contain a wealth of interesting information about where to shoot the seine net, where mullet and smelt are most abundant, which lakes are best for duck, how to get peat or find supplies of driftwood, fresh water and wild celery.

Wind is the principal evil at the Falklands; a region

more exposed to storms, both in winter and summer, it would be difficult to mention . . . 'During the summer, a calm day is an extraordinary event. Generally speaking the nights are less windy than the days, but neither by night, nor by day, nor at any season of the year are these islands exempt from sudden and severe squalls or from gales which blow heavily, though they do not usually last many hours'. Happily there are numerous sounds and bays which form excellent harbours.

The islands were visited by Sir Richard Hawkins in 1594. 'In 1690, Strong sailed through the channel and called it Falkland Sound, after the then Treasurer of the Navy'. It is to be hoped that the compliment resulted in a suitable dividend.

At various times settlements were founded by French, Spaniards and English, but it was only in 1833 that the group was finally taken possession of by Great Britain.

The country consists of tracks of moorland, rocky ridges, hills and mountains, rising to nearly three thousand feet. The soil is of peat, and in the southern spring and early summer, the ground is covered with sweet-scented flowers. 'On some of the hillsides are peculiar streams of stones or fragments of quartz, which appear to flow down into the valleys. They may be twenty to thirty feet in width, and the stones are from one to four cubic feet in size.'

Sheep farming is the main industry. Though none

grow on the islands, the southern shores are covered with trees which have drifted from Tierra del Fuego or Staten Island, and in some of the bays, portions of Fuegan canoes have frequently been found.

Geese, duck and snipe are plentiful and there are trout in the lakes. The Falkland snipe (*Scolopax frenata*) is a solitary bird as large as a woodcock. Formerly seals and sea-elephants were abundant, but indiscriminate slaughter has had the usual result.

Penguins may be seen and heard as much as three hundred miles off the islands, and this has often caused much anxiety to mariners, who imagined that they must be close to land. The cormorant is a much more reliable aid to Navigation, as it is rarely seen more than ten miles off shore.

The dependencies of the Falklands are South Georgia, the South Orkneys, the South Shetlands, the South Sandwich Islands and Graham Land. South Georgia is in the same latitude South as is the Lake District in the North, but except for some tussock grass the island is almost entirely barren, and the south western side is always frozen. It was discovered by Anthony La Roche in 1675 but it was not until one hundred years later that Captain Cook took possession of it.

The South Sandwich group of islands contain active volcanoes. Being of little use for whaling, they are seldom visited, which is only to be expected since they afford no shelter and have no vegetation.

After thinking about these other bleak islands scattered in the lonely southern ocean, the Falkland Islands seemed almost like an oasis to us, but having once passed them, we derived a smug satisfaction from having sighted no land since leaving Australia.

CHAPTER XI

EASTER AT SEA

EASTER brought some disappointment, for the crew had hoped to spend Friday and Monday, the two extra holidays, in reasonably warm weather, but the calm off the Falkland Islands had defrauded them of this. But there were compensations. Heavy rain fell all Thursday night, and as the rain water came off the sails on the foremast, and ran into the forecastle scuppers, it had been carefully collected in tubs in the well-deck, until enough had been saved to fill the small tank, which is the main supply of water for the crew to wash their clothes with. Otherwise, as their daily allowance of water from the ship's tanks is less than a gallon a man, and as the cook takes three-quarters of this, personal cleanliness depends principally on rain.

Good Friday, or Long Friday as it is called in Scandinavia, brought a change of weather. The rain stopped early, and for a few hours the sun shone brightly, though without much warmth. In honour of the occasion, some of the crew, who were old enough to need it, shaved or trimmed their beards. Several amateur barbers were busy with queer looking scissors.

It was then that another large whale put in an appearance, making its first blow so close to the ship that the spray fell on deck. It was a blue whale, and for several hours it cruised slowly around the ship, sometimes passing close under the bowsprit, much to the benefit of a battery of cameras.

All day the wind was light, which made the captain very depressed at the probability of a really slow voyage. The only balm we could offer was that perhaps he would have one less Baltic cruise during the summer.

As an antidote to the holidays, Saturday was devoted to the sailor's anathema — cleaning paintwork. To have wet hands for hours in bitterly cold weather is bad enough alone, but when there is strong caustic in the water, it becomes misery. Finger-nails turn black all over and skin comes off even the horniest hands.

At half-past three on Saturday afternoons work ceases, except for any that is required by the sailing of the ship. For an hour before the evening meal the captain's shop opens, and any of the crew who wish, may come aft to buy soap, duty free cigarettes and matches, their purchases being debited against pay accounts. Some captains sell slops, as clothes are called by sailors, and others spirits as well, though this is bad luck on a ship's company of boys. In one such ship the sailmaker, who was an oldish man and married, used to have his shopping instincts so stimulated by a drink, that he arrived home after one nine month's voyage round the world with eighteen pairs of trousers, a frequently quenched thirst, but no money whatever. When spirits are obtainable from the captain, it is not uncommon for all the forecastle to be drunk on a Saturday night, which must increase the chances of an accident enormously, should any work have to be done aloft.

But this Saturday evening was peaceful and very beautiful for there was a full moon and a clear cold sky. The ship slid slowly through the shining waters with the moonlight reflected off each white yard so that it looked like a bar of silver.

The night brought a phenomenal and most unexpected change of sea temperature, for at 8 p.m. it was 43° F., at midnight 48° F., and at 4 a.m. 56 °F., all in a run of little over forty miles.

By Sunday morning some wind had arrived, and the ship was close-hauled, doing nearly ten knots, with water pouring over the lee bulwarks of the well-deck and spurting in through the freeing ports, as she heeled to the squalls.

This was All Fool's day, which we found is also observed in Scandinavia. The young steward made good — or rather full — use of it, for at an early hour, he told the girl apprentice that she was wanted by a passenger who was notorious for late rising. Worse still, having heard that the enthusiastic third mate had taken eleven star sights the previous evening, the steward told him that the captain wanted the results as soon as possible. The third mate being a very thorough, if slow, worker, it was afternoon when the captain was astonished to receive enough sheets of carefully worked calculations to make a new spanker.

As the wind continued freshening during the day, the lurches to leeward became fiercer so that by 9 p.m. it was time to furl the royals. We had probably been able to carry these longer than any of those ships with only short poops and forecastles, for men working in our well-deck would certainly have been up to their necks in water most of the time. As it was, in *L'Avenir* the watch was dry except for occasional showers of spray. The little struggling figures securing the billowing sails high up on the royal yards showed black against the moon-bright sky, and made a most vivid picture.

Very early the next morning the upper topgallants were furled and during the forenoon of Easter Monday, instead of having a holiday, the watch were employed in furling the lower topgallants. The wind continued to head us all the time, and with the heeling decks wet with rain, it was impossible to keep one's feet without holding on to something.

The sails on the fixed yards are always more difficult to furl than those where the yard is lowered. In the former case, the weather buntlines are hauled taut first, and then the weather clewlines haul the clew of the sail up to the yard, the same process being then employed for the lee half of the sail. This part of the work is, of course, done from the deck, then two or three men go aloft to each sail to pass the gaskets which will secure the furled sail to the yard. Most of the boys are well equipped with oilskin coats, trousers, and seaboots, but in spite of these encumbrances they move about aloft with wonderful agility.

Then came a surprise. During the forenoon and until the moment that the lower topgallant sails had been furled, and the hands had come down on deck, the glass had been falling. It then began to rise appreciably, and in a moment the wind backed round 12 points — 135°. It was an amazing sight to watch the new wind blowing back the spray off the crests of the waves caused by the original wind. Unhappily for the men of the afternoon watch, the wind eased and they spent their holiday afternoon making all sail that had been so carefully furled only a few hours before. Here the moving yards caused the hardest work owing to their weight, for even the upper topgallant yards must weigh about two tons each. They are hoisted by tackles, the falls of which are brought to the nearest capstan. It takes an incredible number of turns of the capstan to get each yard up, so that one gets quite giddy during the process. Both the captain and mate added their weight to the bars, and the knowledge that the wind was now fair and driving us towards warmer weather helped to lighten the labour.

CHAPTER XII

A SAILING SHIP'S RIGGING—
TACKING SHIP

In a book about a voyage in a sailing ship there must of course be included a certain amount of seamanship with its own peculiar language. While it is hoped to keep this down to a reasonable minimum, it must not be thought that either rigging or the manipulation of sails is one of the black arts, only to be understood by those who have made themselves over, body and soul, to the service of the sea.

The rigging for each one of the eighteen square sails is similar, and it is only the appalling total number of ropes which make a sailing ship appear so hopelessly complicated. The ropes are in exactly the same relative positions on each mast, so that a man can put his hand instantly on any rope required even during the darkest night. There is one rule general in sailing ships, that those ropes which always have a heavy strain on them, i.e. halyards and sheets, are only to be touched by the mates.

A brief description of one mast and its sails will suffice. Details can be seen in sketches and photographs.

Three of the six yards on the mast are slung from the

middle by a heavy chain, while the other three are
hoisted and lowered by halyards, the yard being
secured to a crance iron or ring, which slides up and
down the mast. With a strong wind abaft the beam,
if a halyard is let go, the pressure of the wind on the

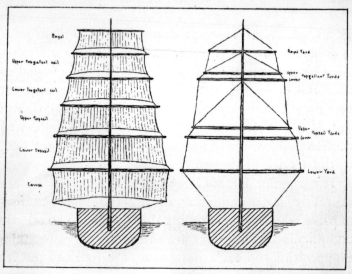

Diagrams to show the yards on a mast which can be lowered and hoisted by halyards

sail will only allow the yard to come down quite
slowly, although it may weigh several tons.

Each sail is secured along its top edge to an iron
rail along the upper forward side of the yard to which
it belongs; when furled, it is bundled up to the same
yard, and ropes called gaskets are passed round sail
and yard.

The sail is spread or set by sheets, generally short lengths of chain tailed to wire rope, which haul out its lower corners to the yardarms (or ends) of the yard below. To furl the sail, clewlines lift the corners when the sheets have been eased, while buntlines lift the foot of the sail up to the yard. As all these ropes lead down

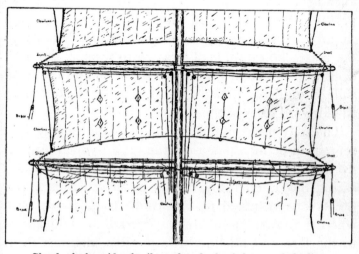

Sketch of after side of sails to show leads of sheets and clewlines.
Foot ropes are only shown on the lower of the two yards

to the deck, unless anything should get foul, there is no necessity for anyone to go aloft, until the time comes to pass the gaskets.

The mast is prevented from falling over sideways by heavy wires called shrouds. Ratlines are short lengths of rope, secured horizontally between the shrouds, so as to form rungs or steps, by which means men can climb aloft; as it is customary not to renew ratlines until they break, it is essential to hold on to the shrouds and not the ratlines when going up or down, so that if one should carry away under one's feet, one's hands will at least have a safe grip.

As the force of the wind is trying to push the ship ahead the masts have a tendency to fall forward. To prevent this, a forest of wires called backstays lead slightly aft to the ship's side from various heights up the mast. Forestays lead forward to support the mast from that direction when tacking, or should the wind shift so suddenly that the wind pressure is exerted on the forward sides of the sails.

The only other important parts of the rigging that remain to be mentioned are the braces which lead aft from each yardarm, so that by hauling on one and easing the other, the yard can be slewed round, and the sail be trimmed to the wind. In *L'Avenir*, from when the lower yards are square, i.e. at right angles to the fore and aft line, it is possible to brace them through an angle of 52° before they touch the backstays. When close hauled, each yard is braced round a little less than the one below it so that the strain on the rigging exerted by the higher sails is proportionately reduced. When the ship is too close to the wind, the highest sails will begin to lift or shake first; therefore the helmsman watches the royals and keeps them just full.

Tacking in a sailing vessel is of sufficient interest to merit a short description.

[*facing:* White sails and the tracery of the rig
Looking aft from the fore

Let us suppose that the ship is close hauled on the starboard tack, yards on the backstays, about seven points off the wind. Both watches are required for the evolution, and even then the mainsail and the cross-

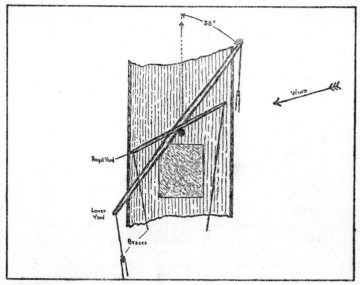

Looking down on one mast to show the angle which the lower and the royal yard can be braced round to, when the ship is close-hauled

jack, in ships which carry square ones, will be clewed up, as there will not be enough men to handle their sheets and tacks quickly enough at the critical moment. The mate stands by the lee main braces while his watch man the weather main braces. The second mate and his watch are similarly disposed at the mizen braces.

The wheel is put over, and the captain watches the compass until the ship has swung through five points up into the wind, when he shouts the order to brace round; the ship's head being then of course only 2 points ($22\frac{1}{2}°$) off the wind. The main and mizen

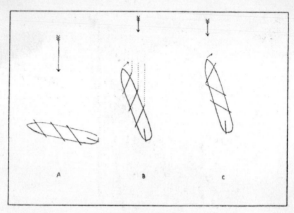

Tacking Ship

A.   Ship close hauled on the starboard tack
B.   Critical moment when lee main and mizen braces should be let go.   Dotted lines show bands of wind acting on the weather parts of these sails
C.   Immediately after the main and mizen yards have been swung round.   Ship continues to turn to starboard

lee braces are carefully coiled down so that immediately the mates throw off the turns securing them, they fly through the blocks as the yards swing round under the force of the wind acting on those parts of the weather yardarms which are not blanketed by the sails on the foremast. This will be clear from the sketches. As the main and mizen yards swing round, the respective watches haul in the slack of their braces at full speed. During this time the ship's head is still swinging to starboard under the influence of the sails on the foremast aback, and will continue to do so even after the way is lost. As soon as the ship's head has well passed the wind, all the hands man the starboard forebraces and haul round the foreyards.

The art of going about lies in giving the order to brace round at the correct moment, for in a fresh breeze, if it is given too early when too much of the weather main and mizen yards are exposed to the force of the wind, they will swing round dangerously fast, and may carry away the backstays. On the other hand if the ship is head to wind or nearly so, the sails on the foremast will so completely blanket the main and mizen, that all the yards will have to be hauled round laboriously, instead of going round on their own. It is dangerous to tack in a very strong wind, as too big a strain would be brought on to the forestays while the wind is acting on the forward side of the sails. Should it be blowing too hard to tack, a ship must wear, i.e., go about stern to wind.

When heaving-to to pick up a pilot and so on, the sails of the foremast are kept full while those on the main, and probably the mizen as well, are kept aback. Of course when running before a gale, the upper sails would have to be clewed up, depending on the strength of the wind, before it would be safe to round up.

Braces are watched carefully, and there is never

enough slack to enable the heavy yards to move more than an inch or two. On one occasion in the *Herzogin Cecilie*, all the forebraces carried away more or less at the same time, and as she was either close hauled, or only just free, the yards swung round on her backstays which for some time were in imminent danger of carrying away. The wheel was put down, and fortunately she answered the helm, and ran off before the wind; at the same time the halyards were let go and sails were clewed up. It must have been a most unpleasant job out on the yardarms shackling on new braces, with the yards free to swing round as they liked.

The *Herzogin Cecilie* has had many exciting adventures, and although she usually gets through them safely, she would hardly be called a lucky ship. On another voyage she was running before a gale with everything set when one of the wires from the midship steering wheel to the rudder parted. She was going so fast, that long before they could change over to the after wheel, she flew up into the wind. Perhaps 'flew' implies too much speed, as any big ship takes an appreciable time to come round. Fortunately for her, when she was broadside on to the wind, the sails blew themselves to pieces, so that by the time the wind got on the foreside of the sails, too few were left to dismast her.

CHAPTER XIII

THE CAPTAIN, PERCY GRAINGER AND THE MATE

THE captain of *L'Avenir* was Nils Eriksson, a nephew of the owner; he was thirty-six years of age, tall, stout, and always cheerful, except during a prolonged calm when he would threaten to become a farmer. He was most courteous and could not have been more thoughtful for our comfort. Not only was he excellent company, but he was most generous in sharing his knowledge and experience of sailing ships.

Besides many years in sail, he has served in steamers, and also in an ice-breaker, which belonged to Abo, and was employed in keeping open a channel from there to Stockholm. This ship had an overhanging bow and a propeller at each end. Her plan of action was to take a good run at the ice, so that the stem would slide well up over it; then as soon as the forward propeller had sucked away some water from underneath the ice, the weight of the bows would break it through. Her propellers were made of special nickel steel and lasted unexpectedly long. Many of the ships regularly trading in the Baltic have propellers of similar material, but the icebreaker would tow any ship with a phosphor bronze propeller, securing a hawser round the foot of her foremast. In spite of advice one American ship elected to be towed straight from her windlass, which they said would stand any strain. Suddenly there was an awful crack as the windlass was torn out by the roots and went flying across the forecastle.

One autumn when our captain was mate of her, the 4-masted barque *Lawhill* was in a Norwegian port and signed on a crew for the voyage to Australia and back. It so happened that none of them had been to sea before except for a couple who had been for a voyage or two on board small ships trading in the Baltic.

As soon as *Lawhill* got into the North Sea, she encountered a very bad gale, which reduced the raw crew to such a state of sea sickness that they rolled wretchedly about in the scuppers or anywhere. No amount of kicking by the mates produced anything but the hope that it might prove rapidly fatal. There was therefore nothing to be done but wait; luckily it was blowing from the southward, so with plenty of sea room the ship ran dead before it. One by one the sails blew out; when at last the wind did ease they had lost sixteen. When the gale had moderated and the crew had been hazed into showing some interest in life, a start was made to sort out fresh sails from the sailroom. While there, the mate sent up one of the most intelligent looking of the crew to loose the mainsail, which was one of the few sails which had been saved. A few minutes later there was an awful roar from the captain, which could be heard all over the ship. When the mate rushed on deck to see what had happened, he found the mainsail hanging in the bunt-lines. The boy had 'loosed the sail' quite literally, having cut as well as the gaskets the stops securing the head of the sail to the yard.

In 1933, the owner decided to use *L'Avenir* for summer cruises in the Baltic, instead of leaving her in peace at Mariehamn between voyages. These cruises are the captain's nightmare, for seventy-five passengers (there is now accommodation for one hundred) come on board to have a good time. Besides various small inside cabins with four bunks, some sleep inside the hatches, one being used for men and another for girls, and some appear not to sleep at all.

Cruises start at Mariehamn and end at Stockholm, or vice versa, and in order that the programme shall be maintained, the owner's tug follows or waits at a rendezvous.

A band is hired and this plays in the sailroom for dancing in the evening. Owing to the slope of the sailroom deck, it is necessary to keep on the starboard tack, or else all the dancers would slither down to the lee side. So by 8 every evening, the captain must get the ship into such position that he will have a clear run for several hours without tacking. This latter operation always presents much difficulty for the mates, who have to use all their tact to clear snoring old gentlemen, knitting spinsters and courting couples out of the coiled braces. Otherwise a serious accident might take place as the yards swung round.

The cruises are well patronized, mostly by Scandinavians, and they prefer to sail all the time rather than to anchor off Visby or any other pleasant summer resort. Owing to the liquor restriction in Finland and Sweden, a fully licensed bar adds to the popularity of the cruises. Passengers are not allowed to go aloft.

The crew do nothing but work the ship, keep her clean, and have their photographs taken by amateurs and newspaper correspondents, as they clamber about aloft.

Percy Grainger and his charming Swedish wife had come out to Australia in *L'Avenir* and had been a great source of interest to the captain and everyone on board. Mr. Grainger is a vegetarian, which is perhaps just as well, for even without meat his energy is phenomenal. We were told that he would be aloft for exercise every day at 5 a.m. and playing deck tennis at 6 a.m. whenever the weather was fine enough. He thought nothing of jumping down on deck from the top of the deckhouse, and his wife said that he had jumped out of a third story window. New York must have an awful fascination for him. He had an odd habit when picking up anything from the ground or deck, for instead of stooping down in the ordinary way, he would bend backwards and pick it up behind him.

Mr. Grainger is a Socialist in theory and in practice, being intensely economical in some directions in order to be completely generous in others. Several times he played the piano for the benefit of the crew, although this must have been torture to him as the instrument had not survived the damp and was therefore completely out of tune. Not by any means a big man, it is told of him that at some railway station in the United States, when a huge negro porter took up his suitcases, Mr. Grainger said, 'Stop, give me that one, it is too heavy for you.' While on a concert tour in the States, after the performance was over, refusing all hospitality, he would often carry his bags to the station and wait there for hours and hours till the next train, saying that he was fond of railway stations.

Mr. Grainger devoted hours each day to writing a book. Perhaps writing is contagious because there was on board at the same time a Dutch lady who began writing letters indefatigably the moment *L'Avenir* left Copenhagen for Australia. All day long her typewriter would be clicking busily. The small post office at Port Victoria must have been overwhelmed when her three months accumulation of well over one hundred letters was posted.

Mrs. Grainger was an artist and was also said to have written verse. She left some attractive oil paintings on board *L'Avenir*, one of them being a large canvas of the captain, standing up with his cat Frassie in his arms. It was excellent of the captain, but Frassie reminded one of Tenniel's Cheshire cat.

The good-looking chief mate, aged twenty-six, was a very fine type of officer. Hard-working and scrupulously just, he was both admired and liked.

There cannot be many other people alive who have been dismasted twice in the same ship, as has happened to him. The ill-fated vessel was *Hougomont*, and it was on her last voyage that he was second mate of her. The passage out to Australia began badly, for to reach Dover from London took thirty days during which they were blown all over the North Sea. After that they did well, for in seventy-two days from Dover they were only about three hundred and fifty miles from Cape Borda, at the entrance to the Spencer Gulf.

It was here that fate dealt them an almost mortal blow. There was a heavy swell, and being in sand ballast, the ship rolled heavily. There was also a rising wind. When the second mate came on watch at midnight, all the royals had been furled, and also both the fore-topgallants and the mizen upper topgallant, as all these latter were beginning to split. Seeing a black squall approaching, the second mate called the captain and got permission to furl the other topgallant sails as well. But before the men had come down from the mizen upper topgallant yard the squall arrived. Though not a very fierce one, when

The Captain, holding Frassie, with the Mate

added to the effect of heavy rolling, it was enough to bring the masts down in fairly quick succession from forward. That the foremast went first was confirmed by the 'policeman' who had gone forward to strike the bell. When the foretopmast crashed down he rushed aft, and was close by the main and then by the mizen mast as each went.

The foremast buckled over just above the lower shrouds, the mainmast broke off six feet above the deck, and the mizen half way up the topmast. The amazing thing was that only one of the main lower shrouds and backstays carried away. The remainder were stretched bar-taut across the deck. The main danger to the ship was from the fore topmast which, with the top gallant mast, was hanging somehow by the topmast fid, and was crashing into the ship's side with each roll. Somehow or other this was lassoed, then the weight was taken by a tackle while the fid was removed and rigging cleared away so that the topmast and topgallant mast could be shot clear over the side. The seizings of the main shrouds were cut with axes, each one flicking over the side with a ping as the last seizing went. The fore-lower yard buckled near the centre so that the two yardarms rested on deck. By about 3 p.m. on that same day all the dangerous wreckage hanging over the side was got rid of, and a start was made on the jury rig. A stay was secured from half-way along the jibboom to the top of the stump of the foremast and on this was hoisted a staysail upside down; a spare royal yard and sail were also used on the foremast, and staysails were rigged up inside the foreshrouds. A jigger staysail was hoisted, but nothing else aft, presumably because she would not have steered well enough. The crossjack yard was still in existence but one yardarm was cocked up into the air.

"Hougomont" under Jury rig.

While they were getting on with the work several steamers sighted them and closed to offer assistance, but this was refused. No one had been hurt during the dismasting, although four men were on the mizen upper-topgallant yard when it came down. The wind held fair and strong, so that sometimes they made as much as four knots. After just under a week, Cape Borda was sighted, when there came a head wind which drove them out to sea again. The lighthouse keepers on Cape Borda had however seen *Hougomont* and had sent the news to Adelaide. A tug was sent out, but failed to find her. At length the wind shifted again, and eighteen days after being dis-masted, she sailed unaided into semaphore anchorage near Port Adelaide and let go her anchor.

The cost of re-rigging her in Australia would have been about three thousand pounds, which was quite prohibitive. The owner did consider having lower-masts and topmasts put into her in Australia, sailing her home under topsails, courses and staysails, and then putting in the topgallant masts and yards at Mariehamn, using his own resources and the accumu-lation of spare gear which he keeps there. But even that was too costly and *Hougomont* now lies as a break-water, with her plates bright red with rust. But at least she had added a fine page to the history of the sea and had upheld the tradition that somehow or other ships must struggle into harbour unaided, unless they are mortally stricken. There is still Pride of Service to be found at sea.

CHAPTER XIV

PHOSPHORESCENCE, WHALES AND WATERSPOUT

IN 38° S. the sixtieth day ended in a perfect warm starlight night with a stillness which no passenger on board a steamer knows. Yet it was a stillness more of spirit than of fact, for as the ship lifted and fell to the heaving of the sea, it caused water noises like the murmuring of a trout stream, which made one long for the scent of a dew-sprinkled springtime countryside. But we were a thousand miles from land and though it was April, being in the southern hemisphere, for us it was autumn. Sometimes a block would creak or a rope would slap against the canvas far overhead, while when a larger swell than usual disturbed the ship, these noises grew to a chorus of protest.

One large dark cloud hung over the western horizon, but all the rest of the sky was clear. Looking down into the black water, one could only see the shimmering reflections of a few stars. But switching the beam of a powerful electric torch downwards into the sea produced a surprising and marvellous effect. Stimulated into activity by the rays of light from above, hundreds of marine creatures in a wide circle gave off phosphorescent light. Those near the surface appeared small and were perhaps single-celled animals, but deeper down were large shapes glowing faintly, which might have been jellyfish or cuttlefish. The display would only last about four seconds after the light was extinguished, but even a short flash would produce some phosphorescence echoing back from the water.

This power of giving off light is known as bio-luminescence. It is possessed by many marine creatures and is produced by the oxidization of a substance called 'luciferin', which, perhaps surprisingly in view of the name, gives off light without any heat. It is therefore a more efficient form of illumination than can be made artificially. It is impossible to say for certain why these creatures should become luminous, but one may conjecture that the light makes them appear larger than they really are, and thus perhaps protects them from some at least of their enemies. But the whole subject is so shrouded in mystery that it would be a most fascinating field to study.

At dawn on the sixty-second day a large steamer was sighted a long way off to the south-east. She seemed to be heading to the west of north as she passed five or six miles under our stern, disappearing to the westward. She was a large ship with a black hull, a black funnel right aft and white upperworks; as we were in 37° S. 32° W., we came to the conclusion that she might be a whale factory or oil tanker returning from the Antarctic whaling grounds.

How could any sane person prefer to travel in a

steamer, where the next port is the main consideration and topic of conversation, directly the last one has been talked out? Excepting in rare moods 'getting there' means nothing to us, leaving the senses free to enjoy the road, with time to sit by the wayside and to watch its changing beauties.

In 33° S., between the extremes of bitter cold in the south and the heat of the tropics, life became as nearly perfect as one's desire for fresh food would permit. Sea of sapphire, blue sky overhead, a fresh breeze on the beam and all round the horizon mountains of billowy clouds, higher and whiter even than our towering royals. One's eye following along the top of the cloud ridges brought to mind the day years ago when the dazzling peak of Teneriffe was first seen in the far distance, thrust up unbelievably high through the ceiling of the clouds.

For a time we lay in the sun in the net stretched beneath the bowsprit, looking down into the clear blue depths and listening to the water sounds. For a second or two, as the bows rose, there would be just a whisper; then as the stem dropped in the swell there would be a hissing and a rushing, swelling almost to a roar, as the bow wave tumbled over itself in scrambling eagerness to get out of the way of the graceful hull.

More whales were seen, and it was noticed that they would often keep station on *L'Avenir* in a regular manner. Can they have tram-like mentalities? From aloft one could watch how, for an hour at a time, one would go round in a wide circle, coming up to blow again and again in the same position in relation to the ship. After some time on the starboard quarter, it would perhaps decide suddenly to change its station to the port beam; where it would carry out the same routine; whatever the speed of the ship, the escorting whale would always move slightly faster. We could not find a satisfactory explanation for the peculiar movements of whales, nor decide why they should find pleasure or profit in keeping company with the ship. Do we give a feeling of protection to the poor great things, or do we stir up the plankton on which they live into an agreeable porridge? The latter theory is hardly tenable as they rarely follow directly astern of a ship.

The modern whale is the largest creature which has ever existed on our world. Whales, also porpoises and dolphins, are warm-blooded, air-breathing mammals, having descended from terrestrial species which have adapted themselves to an aquatic mode of life. In the front flippers of a whale are typical leg bones ending in small bones similar to human hands or feet. In some types, just where the back legs should begin are to be found remnants of bones which now serve no apparent purpose. The temperature of the blood of marine mammals varies from normal to bad influenza, changing little whether they are in the tropics or in the ice-cold waters round the Poles. Hair is one of the main characteristics of mammals, its purpose being to keep the blood warm. Though the whale may have a few fine bristles near the mouth, it is the blubber, or thick coating of fat, which prevents the heat from being dispersed into the sea. A consideration of the portly figures of Channel swimmers makes one wonder if suitable inter-marriage could perhaps produce a human submarine.

Whalebone whales feed by taking in a gulp of water together with the thousands of minute animals which form the plankton or drifting life of the ocean; then with mouth closed raising the tongue forces the water through the whalebone or baleen sieve on which remain the animals ready to be swallowed. The sperm whale has a lower jaw well armed with teeth, for it feeds on giant cuttlefish and squid, which sometimes have tentacles over thirty feet long, and larger round than a man's thigh. The common porpoise and the dolphin belong to the group of toothed whales.

When harpooned a whale can remain under water without breathing for at least an hour, and may 'sound' as deep as half a mile.

Some of the products of whales are used in unexpected ways. The oil obtained by rendering down the blubber may find its way into soaps and candles; the meat is used for human consumption and the scrap remains are made into fertilizers. Sperm blubber makes valuable lubricating oil, while what is left when refined is the spermaceti, utilized in making face creams and cosmetics. The sperm whale also produces ambergris, that precious ingredient of fine perfumes. Though it comes from the intestines, ambergris is more usually found floating in the sea or washed up ashore.

Without doubt whales must follow the trend of ladies' fashions with acute interest.

Towards the end of one fine and warm forenoon during which the ship had made but little headway in a light breeze against a swell, dark clouds began to bank up on the southern horizon. Scattered rain squalls passed on each side of us, bringing puffs of wind from different directions. As the main cloud masses approached from astern, the sea became an ominous indigo colour.

The captain stood aft looking intently for signs of wind on the surface of the water. Suddenly he pointed abeam to starboard, and then blew three staccato blasts on his whistle to call up all hands. Only a few hundred yards away was a large column of light-coloured vapour showing clear against the sombre clouds into which its upper end merged; the darker lower end disappeared into the water in a mass of spray. This was a waterspout and it was dangerously near us. Apart from the fierce whirlwind that keeps it rotating, the spout must contain such a huge weight of water that if it should cross over the ship and break, severe damage at least would be caused.

Shouted orders, the quick movements of the men,

and coils of rope being thrown clear, produce an effect of confusion, especially when heavy rain is splashing down on deck. In actual fact it was only a few minutes before all the royal and upper topgallant yards had been lowered and the sails clewed up, the flying jib, jigger staysail, and jigger topsail had been lowered and the spanker brailed up.

The rain had been so heavy that it had blotted out the waterspout, and prevented us watching its movement. When the rain had eased slightly it was nowhere to be seen, having either moved away fast, or been broken up by the deluge.

Several sailing ships have been struck by waterspouts and have survived to give accounts of the damage. Of two that were thrown over on their beam ends, one had to cut away the main mast in order to right herself. One barque lost all her yards, and another, which was under full sail, was struck without any previous warning, and was completely dismasted below the heads of the three lower masts.

It is impossible to estimate the effect of a waterspout on a modern sailing vessel, and we had no desire to experiment with ourselves. As usual after any emergency was over, there was an immediate return to normality. The watch below was sent down dripping wet to snatch a quick meal of pea-soup and pancakes before turning to for the afternoon watch, while the watch on deck started to set sail once more.

CHAPTER XV

MODELS, CRAFTS, AND BOOKS

IT is a tradition that models shall be made during a long voyage, and accordingly when once the industry had been started, it thrived on board *L'Avenir*.

The mysterious full-rigged ship in a bottle, with a background of church and windmills, has largely gone out of fashion, perhaps because the modern sailor is younger and takes less pleasure in handling a bottle even when empty. The ship is of course completely rigged before being put into the bottle, the masts being so made that they will hinge towards the stern. All the forestays on each mast are led out of the hull or through the bowsprit, so that they can be operated from outside the bottle. The sea and land are made from suitably coloured putty and when this is in place the masts are laid back as flat as necessary so that the model can be pushed through the neck of the bottle. It must be left for a few days while the putty hardens, great care being taken to see that none of the loose rigging gets set into the putty. When all is firm, the stays are hauled taut, fixed with a spot of seccotine where they leave the hull, and are cut off short when dry. Obviously when once the ship is inside the bottle, it is practically impossible to rectify any mistakes.

The best model of all was one of *L'Avenir* on a scale of one-sixteenth of an inch to a foot. It was made from red pine and a remarkable assortment of odds and ends, including a toothbrush of the captain's which had been superseded at a convenient moment. The rigging was all made from strands of wire unlayed from flexible electric cable. This could be twisted up either

Ship model to be put in a bottle, showing how stays are brought out through the hull and bowsprit to set up the hinged masts

double or treble, as required, with an ordinary hand drill. The difficulty of getting the stays and shrouds taut was solved by bringing them down through the hull and out of the bottom of the ship where they could be pegged. The blocks, about one hundred and forty of them were made of silver paper over a little frame of wire. The figurehead was the only thing which was definitely not *L'Avenir's*. She was obviously a lady, and having a lovely pair of goo-goo eyes we suspected that she was a portrait. This model had to face a fierce fire of criticism for everyone thought it almost a duty to point out some mistake.

There were four other models of *L'Avenir*. They were all more heavily sparred, but in all the rigging had to be exactly correct. The Elizabethan galleons had a distinct advantage in that they could be made for beauty rather than accuracy, for since there were no available books or plans of ships of the period, it was easy enough for the builders to turn aside any criticism.

There was also a model of the well-known cutter *Jolie Brise*, heroine of several Fastnet races. This was a first effort, and was done mainly with a knife. Enormous trouble was taken to get the lines correct, and at one stage the hacked and wounded piece of timber was covered with ink on one side and blood on the other. Rudders broke so frequently that spare ones were finally made by mass production. Carried away by the urge to incorporate a toothbrush, a tiller was made out of one of such a repulsive pink colour, that public opinion united to have it scrapped.

With so many dockyards working at full pressure, some raw materials became scarce. The wood of cigar boxes was in great demand, for it could be cut very thin with a fretsaw. Pins became so precious that even bits of them were hoarded. For metal work, toothpaste and shaving cream tubes were found useful. Decks could be made to look as if they were planked by forcing black cotton into seams made by a knife cut, and then varnishing the whole surface.

Requiring some thread of rope colour for rigging, we asked the steward to dye some white stuff in coffee. Presently he brought along a fearful brew, steaming in a sausage tin, and told us with pride that it was a mixture of tea, coffee, cocoa, Worcester sauce, vinegar and mustard, which were all the brown and yellow ingredients he could think of. The result was excellent when the smell wore off.

Once the hulls had been chiselled out, a sharp knife or razor blade was found to be the model maker's most useful tool, though drills are of course essential. The smallest ones were made from needles with the eye broken off and the end ground on four sides until a point was produced.

It was interesting to note how the different temperaments of the model makers were expressed. One would paint and fix each detail in place directly it was finished, while another would postpone taking any such irrevocable step until the very last possible moment, by which time some vital piece probably had to be remade, having got lost or been taken away by the kitten. One of the galleon makers had gay coats of arms on the hull, and tin sails bellying to the wind, ornamented with bright designs, before any of the lower rigging was in place. He was quite frank about the quality of his work, and said he knew the exact dark corner at home where it would act as a decoration and yet be able to avoid being examined too closely.

Except for the large amount of time it takes, model making has much to recommend it apart from any result. Not being messy, it can be quite a social occupation, and as there is always a variety of different details which can be tackled according to mood, it need never become monotonous. Whether the more or less technical knowledge that one inevitably gains is of any direct use is doubtful, but it certainly gives an added pleasure to books about the days of sail.

Besides models, there were many other handicrafts practised, some inspired by interest, others by necessity. For it must be remembered that the only real craftsman on board were the sailmaker, the carpenter (or 'timmerman' in Swedish) and the donkeyman, who is the ship's metal worker, so that although they were willing to give help and advice, people who wanted anything done always tried to do it themselves.

The first complete piece of work was a star globe, a device which provides the simplest means by which the navigator can identify a star of which he has taken a sight. The hardest part of the problem was to make a globe out of a lump of timber without a lathe or any suitable tool except a chisel. After the corners of the original cube were taken off, more and more corners were cut off until there were dozens and dozens of facets of differently shaped quadrangles and triangles. Sand-paper smoothed off the whole, and after it had been inked over to give a suitable night effect, the celestial meridians were marked by wires let into the surface of the wood and the stars were represented by small brass nails.

Many useful and ornamental things were made out of sennit, a sort of glorified plaiting which has many variations. Three or four fathoms of sennit could be coiled round and sewn so as to make a perfect sole for a hot-weather slipper, the uppers being of canvas. The sailmaker knew a very complicated and difficult Turkish sennit which he made into beautiful mats. A round sennit of coloured twines with a flat wooden anchor at one end and a hogsback eye at the other made an attractive belt for a girl.

Books about the sea were much more popular than one would expect during a voyage. Though *Ship Ashore* could hardly be classed as one of these it was generally considered the most fascinating book on board, not only because salvage must appeal to everyone, but because of the countless good stories which the author, Desmond Young, has woven in so naturally that they seem part of the texture. He points out that one of the main attractions of salvage is that each job is completely different in everything, except that every one requires unremitting hard work, constant watchfulness and attention to detail. The element of luck comes into the problem through weather and greater hidden damage or strain than can be discovered at the beginning of operations. It must be this variety which makes 'wreckers' the interesting characters they are. It would be hard to imagine more ingenuity than was shown by the engineer who, to pay off an old score on a diver, managed to slip in a bluebottle into the latter's helmet just before the face piece was screwed on and he went down.

Mr. Young was especially enterprising and wise to get clear of the army quickly, and to take full advantage of the short interval after the War before the world became sub-normal. His yarns against the navy and their attempts at salvage never leave the slightest trace of bitterness, nor can Americans take offence at his suggestion that the Shipping Board was 'a gift', considering that for a time a correspondence course in navigation was said to be sufficient qualification for command of one of their ships.

Whether or not this is true, either these correspondence courses must be very good or Alan Robinson must be a remarkable pupil, for he started off with no practical experience at all and sailed round the world in a tiny ketch called *Svaap*. Most of the way he had a crew of one, a cheerful Tahitian, who was a first class seaman but had all the traditional failings of a sailor in harbour, invariably getting himself locked up. The book, *Deep Water and Shoal*, is even better than Ralph Stock's *The Cruise of a Dream Ship*. It is delightful reading, either as a travel book or from the sailing point of view, between which he has struck a perfect balance. Some parents will keep the book under lock and key, for Mr. Robinson, while in the twenties, threw up his business and sank every penny of his savings in *Svaap* and her equipment, with the determination of getting round the world and living on what he could make out of an untried pen.

Of the other occupations on board during spare time, learning English was one of the most common as it has to be studied during courses at the Finnish navigation schools. The Swedes say that English is a very nice language indeed, except that when you want to say 'Babylon' you pronounce it 'Nebuchadnezzar'. Incidentally they think that Danish sounds like a child trying to talk Swedish with a mouthful of hot potato. By the end of a hard day's work, the boys had little physical energy left to spare, but on Sundays in fine weather, gymnastics and feats of strength were often practised on the forecastle head.

Oddly enough, the only serious accident which occurred on board was a result of model making; while carving out a hull, one of the crew drove a chisel into his thigh.

CHAPTER XVI

TAKEN ABACK AND CHANGING SAILS

THE sixty-fifth was a warm muggy day with a fresh easterly wind and heavy showers of rain. The ship was heeling well over to port as we were close-hauled on the starboard tack. During the afternoon the wind had shown a tendency to head us gradually. The captain, who had been suspecting that the wind might shift quickly, had remained on deck almost continuously. He was talking to us in the chart house, when suddenly, without a word, he sprang up and was out on deck before the ship came upright. For in a moment the wind had backed eight points (90°) and had taken us aback. The helmsman had put the wheel to port to try to catch up to the wind, but the captain immediately ordered it to be reversed, having decided to go about, not only because the new tack would bring us nearer our desired course, but to spend as short a time as possible in an unpleasant predicament. For when sailing fast with a fresh breeze, to be taken aback is one of the most dangerous things which can happen to a sailing ship, as the wind on the wrong side of the sails may put an enormous strain on the forestay, which the captain refers to with great reverence as 'the heart of the whole rig'. The only immediate remedy may be to let go all the halyards in the hope that the sails will blow out before the masts go.

Luckily for us the change of wind brought heavy rain without any hard squalls. The mizen and main yards were braced right round, the spanker was

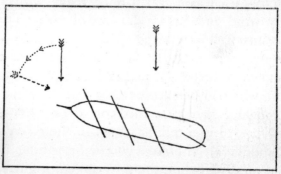

Diagram to show how a sudden shift of wind to ahead takes the ship aback, and acts on the fore sides of the sails

brailed up and the sails on the foremast were left aback, until the ship's head had been blown round enough for the sails on main and mizen mast to fill on the new tack. Then the fore yards were braced round and the spanker reset. As might be expected the ship gathered an appreciable amount of stern way, enough to make it necessary to put the wheel hard to port again.

The following day, in 30° S., saw the first of the fair weather sails make their appearance. These are the old, patched and repaired ones, many of them on their last voyage, which are worn out in the trades and doldrums. Only the best sails will stand up to the storms of the southern ocean, or of the North Atlantic in anything but summer.

A spanker, topsail or course made of the heaviest British canvas, with wire roping round the edge, is a weighty thing, so that when it has to be shifted along the deck, it is carried on the shoulders of a line of men, looking like a semi-human centipede. The spanker was the first sail to be changed, then the mainsail, a square one replacing the triangular sail which had brought us from Australia. Both these were relics of the Belgian training days, and the mainsail was fitted with cringles and eyelets for one reef. Excepting in training ships which have large crews, sails are not reefed; as the wind increases whole sails at a time are furled.

While the head of the mainsail was being stopped to the yard, one of the apprentices spent some time kneeling on the extreme yardarm while he used both hands to haul a lashing taut. And yet on some voyages these boys may not go aloft very often. On the way out to Australia *L'Avenir's* royals were only furled two or three times; if it is not necessary to shorten sail, except for shifting a worn-out sail or the whole suit, there may be no reason for a boy to go aloft, as all refitting work is normally done by the able seamen. Just before the mainsail was hoisted up, much amusement was caused when the mate caught sight of a figure aloft, and let out a furious blast: 'What the —— —— are you loafing up there for?' From among the maze of ropes appeared the astonished face of a passenger who had been watching operations with earnest interest.

This was the first day that shirts were generally discarded, white skins appearing that were bronzed when last seen. Presumably prolonged and very cold weather is the worst enemy of fashionable sun-tan. As usual, several of the men working aloft were wearing clogs, which though heel-less, they contrive not to shed on to the mate's head.

Two small fish appeared close under the stern, the first we have seen since leaving Australia. By a strange coincidence, this was the first day that we had had no escort of albatrosses. For a time during the morning, not a single bird was in sight, but later on some petrels arrived.

We were now in the horse latitudes, a region of variable winds between the westerlies and SE trades; this is considered the most difficult and tedious of the calm belts which have to be crossed. On the equator between the SE. and the NE. trades lie the doldrums, and there are more horse latitudes again between the NE. trades and the westerlies of the North Atlantic. Referring to these last horse latitudes, Findlay says that the name is derived 'from the fact that vessels in former years, employed in carrying horses to the West

[*facing:* At work aloft in fine we

Indies, were frequently obliged to throw them overboard, during the embarrassment caused by the continual changes, sudden gusts, and calms, rains, thunder and lightning, which are general in it.'

The Scandinavians have no counterpart to the term horse latitudes but call them doldrums as well.

As we left the Tropic of Capricorn behind, the captain began to get worried about the sails, for the best ones were still bent. There is obvious economy in wearing out and using up old sails; also being softer they are often actually better in light breezes; but the main reason for the change is that good canvas is injured by the tropical sun.

Fresh breezes and the desire to make good use of them, had delayed the shifting in the higher horse latitudes after which regular and heavy showers of rain had kept the new sails constantly damp. As these may not be required for six months, it is essential that they should be stowed away bone dry.

By an old custom, the watch below and the daymen are all turned-to in order to make a quick evolution of the work, which can then be completed in one day. But owing to rain in the night, it took until afternoon on the seventy-second day for the sails to dry, so that it was decided to work on the foremast only, with the watch on deck. This gave the watch below the rare opportunity of being able to sit around on the forecastle and bowsprit, to criticize as freely as the mate's proximity would allow.

All the orders are given in Swedish. Many of them are so similar to English terms that we could understand them. It is quite common for some direction given in Swedish by one of the mates to be interpreted into English by a German lad, for the benefit of a Belgian.

Like flying, efficiency in ground work is vital, for much delay is caused if sails are sent aloft badly made up, or if buntlines, clewlines and so on are not tended exactly as required by those aloft. Usually two at a time, sails are clewed up, the moving yards being lowered first. Then the gantline, a rope rove through a block at the masthead, is passed round the middle of the sail, the clewlines and sheets are secured together and then unshackled from the lower corners of the sail. Next after the buntlines are unrove, the yarns securing the head of the sail to the yard are cut, so that each side of it falls down until the gantline has the weight. Heaving up on the gantline allows the sail to be pushed clear on the fore side of the yards, when it is lowered to the deck. There the old sail is ready to be hoisted up in its place.

Unshackling or shackling the chain sheets provides some good opportunities for acrobatics, and once we saw a lad sitting in the bight of the sail, with one hand on the foot-rope above him apparently unscrewing the shackle that held the sail, but the alarm was a false one for he had passed a rather slender looking lanyard underneath, and was actually sitting on that.

While waiting for the sail to come up, Dirty Peter, a pleasant Belgian lad who always pretended to be lazy, stretched out at full length on the top of a yard, with his hands behind his head. One of *L'Avenir's* previous chief mates, when exasperated by slow work aloft, often used to dash up and run out along the top of a yard like a tightrope dancer, dealing out curses and an occasional kick to the guilty ones.

Hardly a breath of wind stirred the surface of the sea so that the loss of a few sails at a time made no difference. A heavy swell was rolling up from the south, but fortunately we never quite lost steerage way so that, coming up from astern, it did not make us roll unpleasantly. Calm with a swell causes more chafe, wear and tear than a high sea with wind.

For the first time for many weeks we heard the squawks of two seabirds which were chasing each other. They were gone before they could be identified with glasses, but appeared to be Schleigel's petrels. It is extraordinary that such a trivial occurrence as a bird's cry should make any impression, but probably we had never become quite accustomed to the complete absence of noise, except for that made by wind, sea or ship. Seen from aloft the sea was a glorious sapphire and almost luminous in its clearness. Later there were a number of heavy rain squalls around us but none came over us, so that the sails were safely stowed away dry. It would have been cruelly tantalizing had we been short of fresh water. Just before sunset, the sun broke through below a dark leaden coloured cloud, and filled a narrow band above the horizon with molten gold, tinting all our sails orange for a few moments before all the bright colour drained out the sky.

The following morning all hands, including daymen and watch below, were employed changing the sails on the main and mizen masts. Jackie, the girl apprentice, was employed on deck putting into the cringles along the head of each sail the yarns by which they were secured to the yards. Unwittingly she put them in the wrong way round; we hoped she couldn't hear the curses of the men aloft as each sail came up. The stowaway, now called George, having learnt three swear words in Swedish, used them continuously one after the other with great feeling, much to everyone's amusement. By now he was definitely of use aloft, though liable to make mistakes.

During the whole of these two days only one object, a small shackle, was dropped from aloft, and luckily this fell over the side. There was nearly a serious accident when an eyebolt on deck broke off, and a block, which had been hooked to it, shot like a missile from a catapult close by the head of a lad who was backing up the rope round a winch drum.

There was still a very heavy southerly swell which must have been caused by some very fierce storm in

[*facing:* On a yard-arm, high above the shimmerir

the vicinity of Cape Horn. We wondered if *Winterhude* or *Mozart* were down there.

Alongside us in the water was a complete silhouette of the ship shadowed by the strong sun. Every sail was clear cut and some fish darted round them, black in the shadow and green in the sunlight.

CHAPTER XVII

SAILMAKER AND THIRD MATE

DURING the hot weather one of the best places in the ship was the big space in which the cadets used to sling their hammocks, where one could lie on a heap of sails, looking up through the skylight at the blue heavens above, and yarn to the sailmaker.

He was the oldest man on board, and was a most delightful character with a wonderful wealth of experience.

In his young days he sailed for years in Scottish barques — even now he can sometimes be mistaken for a Scot — and has been in barquentines and schooners coasting round England to such places as Par, Teignmouth, Exmouth, and also to Exeter, where ships were towed by a horse up the canal through pleasant green meadows. He once served in a ship on Lake Superior; also in an Australian coaster, which must have had a dull run as he never visited Melbourne, Adelaide or Tasmania.

Spending an evening ashore at the Cape during the Boar War he nearly became a trooper in Methuen's Horse, for a recruiting sergeant tackled him in a bar saying, 'You're a likely looking lad. Can you ride?'

'Only a yardarm,' was the reply, which was not considered good enough for the cavalry.

The sailmaker has nine children and says that there is such a noise when they are all together, that he almost wishes that he was away at sea. One of his brothers is a Doctor of Divinity, and another is a missionary at Shasi, a small port in the Yangtse nearly a thousand miles from the sea. Perhaps this connection with the Church explains the fact that, on festive occasions, the sailmaker argues fluently about religion, being quite ready to support his beliefs with fists.

Also a good carpenter, he is probably the best sailmaker in Captain Eriksson's fleet; yet he is wonderfully generous in teaching the art to his assistants, or to any of the crew who really want to learn. It is a pleasure to watch him work — fortunately for the owner he can talk at the same time — for his speed and accuracy are remarkable. After putting a huge patch down the whole length of the sail, there will not be the slightest trace of a wrinkle anywhere. While his mates occasionally break as many as four needles a day, the sailmaker himself has not broken one for two years. In one day he cut up over a third of a mile of canvas for new sails.

A great reader, preferring travel and adventure to love interest, he has good taste, although he did offer to lend us some awful looking 'audacious' paper backs, such as *Sailors Wives*, which had on the cover a picture of a much made-up girl with an officer's cap and half-closed eyes, holding up a champagne glass. During the Baltic cruises, the sailmaker has a rest from his craft and is in great demand for showing people round the ship and for spinning hair-raising yarns. Being a bit of an artist he always goes right up to the limit of what they can be expected to believe. Such questions as these are asked:

'Have you ever been wrecked?'

'Three times.'

'Oh. And were you saved?'

'The last time I had to come ashore on the kedge anchor.'

Telling us about the young son of a Swedish noble-man who came on board as an apprentice, and wanted to know what time they would bring him his coffee in bed, the sailmaker remarked: 'He was a bit trouble-some at home, so his parents had to send him to sea — or else go themselves.'

The sailmaker's art is of great importance, for if sails are badly cut, they do not last nearly as long. Most ships make a new suit of sails for one mast each round trip, which means that none of the best hard-weather sails should be more than three or four years old. Before they finally blow to pieces in some tropical squall, sails may be as much as ten or twelve years old.

As a general rule a sail can be used in a similar position on any mast. In the ship's plans no less than twenty-five tons is allowed as the weight of *L'Avenir's* sails.

The sailmaker told us how some years ago the four-masted barquentine *M——* had a narrow escape from disaster. Just having changed hands, her first trip was to be from Ostend to Norway, where a cargo of timber was to be loaded. She carried a crew of fourteen.

Her captain, expecting only a three day's trip, had decided that to fill all the water ballast tanks would suffice. But outside in the North Sea, they found to their horror that the ship was so weak that, in any breeze, she lay right over. Before they could make any port in order to obtain some more ballast, a southerly gale sprang up, during which they did not dare hoist even a rag of sail for fear of capsizing.

All the time — this was in February — *M——* was being blown to the northward. Somehow or other the only chronometer was dropped, breaking to pieces so literally, that the steward swept up cog wheels and screws with dustpan and brush. After a fortnight the fresh water gave out, so they lit up the donkey boiler and managed to distil enough for bare necessity. Before long they were drifted north of any chart which they had on board, so that the captain had to pin bits of notepaper on to the top of the most northerly one they could find. After the first bad gale, whenever there were head winds, which there usually were, *M——* dare not carry any sail.

At last the coal ran out, so that to keep the galley

fire going they tore up the wooden between-decks. Luckily before this happened, enough rain had been collected to serve as drinking water. When all the kerosene had been used up, no navigation lights were shown at night, though this mattered but little as they were then so far north that only an occasional trawler could be met with. Tallow was used for lights inside the ship. Almost the only anxiety they were free from was about food, for there was about nine months' supply on board.

At length when they had struggled south and the captain decided he was three hundred miles west of the Shetlands, they met a fishing vessel who told them they were still in the North Sea. After a voyage of two months over unknown seas, the *M*—— crawled into Bergen in Norway and found that her cargo of timber had been shipped long since, and that they had all been given up for lost.

The young fair haired third mate of *L'Avenir* was a Finn, who spoke Swedish so badly that the captain and the other mates could only understand about half of what he said. He had an utterly toneless deep voice with an almost tragic monotony that suggested a stream losing itself in a marsh. This was a great handicap, for besides being an undesirable source of amusement for the men, it was worse than useless for encouragement or for spreading enthusiasm. Such jobs as bracing round the yards took much longer than they should have done.

Being fresh from the navigation school, he took himself very seriously without suspecting that he was a bit of a joke. Early in the voyage he gave up shaving, but very little happened except a few long soft goat-like hairs on his chin which earned him the name of 'Leprecaun'. He had phenomenally long toes, almost as long as fingers. As the weather grew hotter he put on more and more black cardigans, and yet thicker dark serge trousers. His washing sometimes remained on a line on deck for two or three weeks, and if he brought his best blue suit on deck for an airing, it would be certain to pour with rain directly he forgot about it.

As the ship's doctor he was always messing about with the contents of the medicine cupboard, mixing up foul concoctions which at least had the effect of discouraging sickness. One day a couple of the boys invented most hair-raising symptoms and groaned them out to the Leprecaun. Much interested, he told them he had just the right medicine, at least he had nine out of ten necessary ingredients.

The Leprecaun caught the enthusiasm for arts and crafts and started to make a star globe, or rather, the box to hold it in, when he could buy a sphere about the size of a croquet ball. For no apparent reason he made an enormous box, almost big enough for the croquet mallets as well, which, in spite of a coat of something like tar, contrived to warp badly in the humidity of the tropics.

Consequently when he announced his intention of painting a picture, the matter was treated as a huge joke. We were really surprised when the Leprecaun complacently produced a surprisingly good oil painting of the *Archibald Russell* in a gale. The treatment was conventional and some of the work was a little crude, but considering that it was done with the ordinary ship's oil paints, the result was remarkable. It was not long before the artist obtained a patron, who commissioned him to paint a picture of *L'Avenir* in exchange for a pair of sea-boots.

CHAPTER XVIII

SOUTH-EAST TRADES

NAVIGATION would become a really popular pastime if it could be conducted exclusively in the trade winds. A true and steady breeze, glorious blue sea flecked with white caps, warm days and reasonably cool nights make sailors forget their Cape Horn resolution to quit the sea and take up farming. Shirts are abandoned in favour of brown skins, though some of them are still an angry red from being overdone while changing sails.

It was during the south-east trades that our navigation lights were exhibited for the first time since getting clear of Australian waters. No steamers follow our track, and as other sailing ships would be going in the same direction, there would be so little danger of collision, that it was considered justifiable to economize in oil.

The three remaining pigs having taken up residence in their summer sty, were sometimes allowed to roam about in the well deck. The forge was kept there in fine weather and the pigs discovered coal to be a luxury, crunching it with the relish of dyspeptics eating charcoal biscuits. Let us hope that they realized that until the tropics and the hot weather were passed, they were merely pets.

Our pigs had been especially well looked after and were in fine condition unless perhaps they were a shade too fat for the hot weather. Sea-going pigs often come to a bad end. On her last voyage the *Pamir* had two, but one cheated the executioner's knife by committing suicide through a freeing port, when it was too rough to turn round and rescue it, while the other just took sick and died so gruesomely, that even hungry sailors would not eat it. A long voyage without any fresh meat whatsoever must be a trial, though it is quite possible that the moral effect of a couple of pigs is of as much value as the vitamins they possess.

One day the pigs were let out into the well deck at an unfortunate time, and managed to get themselves covered in red lead. The mate was even less pleased about it when we chided him for not having the pigs properly chipped before painting them.

Our chance of adding to the edible livestock vanished as soon as we got N. of South Trinidad Island. For the captain had promised that if he were becalmed within a reasonable distance, we could land to make an attack on the pigs and goats which have run wild there since the last settlers went away. The Ilha da Trinadade, to give it its correct name, is less than three miles long and one and a half miles wide; it lies in 20° 30 minutes S. and 29° 30 minutes W. In 1700 it was taken possession of by the Doctor Halley, who later became Astronomer Royal, and in 1780 an attempt was made, but failed, to form an English settlement there. More recently the Brazilians repeated the attempt, but though it also failed, the island still belongs to Brazil.

It is a rugged heap of rocks rising nearly two thousand feet to the central peak; there is such a constant swell breaking on the iron bound shores that landing on the sharp coral rocks is always difficult. On shore, wherever there is any flat land, it is covered with a rich mould in which grow castor oil plants, acacia bushes and a coarse grass. There are many dead trees and the beaches on the eastern side of the island are covered with planks and timber. Land-crabs infest the island, and many birds nest there, such as petrels, noddies, terns, frigate birds, and red-footed boobies.

Though we passed within about one hundred miles of the island bird life about the ship remained scarce. Occasionally a tern passed by without even appearing to notice the ship, so that we were almost flattered when a blue-faced booby of the gannet family, followed us for a time. On one occasion when fish were breaking surface half a mile away, being harried by larger fish from below, a crowd of screaming terns were making the most of the occasion from above.

One evening a common noddy, a dark coloured tern with a lavender-grey head, perched on the bow-sprit and was captured. When the sailmaker brought it aft to be identified, it savagely bit his forefinger, but the poor simple noddy might as well have chosen a lump of leather, for after forty years of sailmaking, that particular master finger was solid hard skin right through.

Although terns have webbed feet, adult birds do not often settle on the sea, preferring drifting wood or weed if no beach is near enough.

Though over half the different species of sea-birds are to be found in or near the tropics during some part of the year, one may sail these seas for days on end without sighting a single bird beyond the faithful storm petrels. Perhaps the heat saps the vitality of the rest, and turns them into beach combers.

As an offset, there are the woolly trade wind clouds flying across the heavens, and a more lovely colour, as well as greater interest, in the sea. From a sailing ship, one can really see and appreciate the beauty of the Portuguese man-of-war. Its body being almost transparent, the colour of sea beneath is tinted with purple, edged with the red of the delicate frill on top of its back. But like many a beauty, this creature's character leaves much to be desired, for besides stinging, it is not content to remain just a jelly-fish, but aspires to be a non-rigid airship. Unhappily its calculations have not been worked out right for it cannot quite take off. The lovely bladder is filled with gas secreted by a special gland, so that it acts as a sail carrying the Portuguese man-of-war over the ocean, with its tentacles spread below. These latter have powerful stinging cells which paralyse any prey they happen to touch.

One evening during a strong squall while torrents of rain were falling, a blue and white butterfly suddenly appeared. It had a wing span of about three inches, and by using the eddies on the lee-side of the ship it kept in sight for several minutes before being swept helplessly away. As the coast of Brazil was nearly three hundred miles dead to leeward, the arrival of a butterfly took some explaining away. Some said that it had hatched out on board. But above the trade winds there are counter-trades which blow in the reverse direction, and keep up a circulation of air between the tropical and sub-tropical regions. Somehow the butterfly must have got up into the counter-trades and have been blown out to sea until it became involved in the squall which brought it down out of control in our vicinity. Occasionally ships suffer from a plague of insects. One year when *Viking* was off Cape Verde millions of large red locusts swarmed over the ship covering the sails and rigging. It seemed impossible to keep them out of the inside of the ship and they got everywhere. They ate all the captain's geraniums but fortunately they did not relish flax or manilla. For two days they stayed on board, and as they became exhausted, fell down from aloft like hail, so that there was an unpleasant scrunching sound as one walked over the deck.

After this squall, when the third mate went on to the

forecastle he was surprised to find that the flying jib had been 'blast sonder', as the deck log records the blowing out of a sail. It was an old one, patched so many times that it absorbed more weight of rain than it had strength to support.

Towards the end of the SE. trades we passed the latitude of Fernando Noronha which is one of those small, rare and remarkable islands, which rise out of the deep water of the Atlantic. Four and a half miles long and less than two wide the land is hilly and wooded; there is one extraordinary thousand foot hill which appears to lean over and overhang its base on one side.

It is now only used as a penal settlement for the State of Pernambuco; the guards, their families and about eight hundred convicts make a total population of about two-thousand. The convicts work at their own trades, and raise enough Indian corn, cotton, cassava, castor oil and fruits to meet the needs of the island.

Owing to the constant swell, landing is always more or less difficult. It is effected by means of a 'balsa' or raft, with a raised platform, which works on a rope secured between a buoy and the shore. In the dry season water is not plentiful or good, and the Sailing Directions warn the mariner that though wood can be obtained, it is difficult to ship, and is infested with centipedes and other insects.

Many of the nights in or near the tropics are so unbelievably beautiful that they take one's breath away. A sailing ship is always intensely alive, even when ghosting along with only a breath of wind. Though all the sounds are hushed, everything aloft is wide awake and one can distinguish myriads of different voices ranging from groans to squeaks, sighs and the rustle of rope against canvas. As one climbs the weather shrouds one is rewarded with a gallery of pictures of the wonder of the sky and night, each one framed between the curving foot of the dark sail and the silvery yard beneath it.

Far below, the lamp in the chart house spreads a pool of light on to the decks still wet from an earlier shower and the white brace blocks catch up reflections from it. Now and then as he leans forward to check the course, the helmsman's head is silhouetted against the dim light of the binnacle.

At regular intervals, as the swell sweeps along the ship's side, there is a queer scuttering sound as it slaps under an overlapping plate. A faint footfall from the mate on watch, invisible in the darkness below, means perhaps that he is struggling against sleep. Right forward on the forecastle head is the lookout who has to walk backwards and forwards until the small bell struck at the hours and half hours by the helmsman galvanizes him into sudden activity, so that he can strike an echo on the main ship's bell before the mate can suspect him of being sleepy.

Every hour the helmsman and lookout are relieved, when they must report to the officer of the watch. Often the spell of night is so powerful that everyone on deck speaks softly, hardly above a whisper. Sometimes far away out in the darkness comes the sighing of some mammal which has come up to the surface to breathe.

CHAPTER XIX

DOLDRUMS, SHARK, SUCKER FISH, STEAMERS

To many people, the doldrums near the equator probably conjure up a picture of ease and indolence, under cloudless blue skies, with a horizon empty and unbroken all round. In actual fact the doldrums mean a lot of hard work, for though there may be no wind at all for several hours on end, it is more usual to get fickle breezes which only last just long enough for all the yards to be braced round to meet them, when they rudely drop or change direction. Besides the eighteen yards to be braced round, there are the spanker and the tacks and sheets of the courses to be dealt with, besides which the sheets of all staysails may have to be shifted over. It may easily take over half an hour and a great deal of energy for the watch to complete the work.

Heavy rain squalls are the great feature of this region. Huge detached masses of cotton-wool clouds, dazzling white on top and leaden colour below are joined to the sea by the falling rain. Sometimes half a dozen or more squalls may be in sight at the same time. Each one has wind, more or less, near it, so that it is the succession of squalls, and the few miles which each one gives, which must be relied on to get ships through the doldrums. It was the wonderful ghosting qualities of some of the old clippers which helped them to make such fast passages. The flapping of their sails in the long swell would be enough to move them along, and once moving, the sweetness and fineness of their under-water lines offered the minimum of resistance.

The south-east trade wind had been a dismal failure on the whole, both in force and direction. The best day's run which it had given us was only 148 miles, and the wind had on the whole come from the northward of east. In 2° S. it died away altogether. This was the eighty-third day, and just before dawn a large cargo steamer passed us, apparently bound for Pernambuco. She did not come very close, and efforts to exchange signals were frustrated by twilight, which made flashing difficult yet was insufficient to allow flag signals to be read.

A big rat, surprised by daylight, had been seen trotting into our cabin where it got into a hole beside some pipes, underneath the settee. A trap was set with an appetizing meal of bread, cheese and schnapps. The meal went off but not the trap, which was found to be so sticky that all the rats in the ship could have held a dance on it without a moment's anxiety. However the schnapps had evidently given the rat a thirst, for that evening the steward saw it drinking from the folding wash-basin, which he quickly slammed closed with the rat inside. The alarm was given and a strong party assembled, including the captain, so that we could hardly close the cabin door. Josephina the cat was produced, looking rather astounded and put out. Gingerly the basin was lowered, but nothing was to be seen. Then the lower cupboard was opened and out sprang a huge rat. Everyone jumped, someone screamed, and for a moment Josephina flinched. Then in a flash she was under the settee. After a moment's scuffle out she came proudly, with the rat still kicking in her mouth, looking round as if to say, 'where's my damned kitten'.

The day's excitement was not quite over yet, for late in the evening another steamer passed us on the horizon bound to the southward. The captain had decided to cross the equator in 30° W. and as we were going north along this meridian, we were close to the main line of traffic.

Dawn the following morning disclosed to us another sailing ship a long way off on the starboard bow. We were able to identify her as the *Pommern*, as she is the only four-masted barque which does not carry royals. Smoke was also sighted ahead and in course of time a tramp steamer wallowed past us about a mile off — the *Dunely* of Whitby. She did not bother to hoist an ensign, and we thought her lacking in enterprise and thoughtfulness in not coming closer to look at us and to tell us whether the world was at peace. It reminded one of Kinglake's story in *Eothen* of the two travellers who, with their camel caravans, met in the middle of a boundless desert and, being English, passed without a word, only giving each other the Englishman's greeting, a 'curse you, who are you' sort of expression.

It must be admitted that we were disappointed that none of these three steamships should have been near enough or civil enough to ask if we wanted to be reported, for the certainty of a very long voyage made sure that families would be anxious.

With the *Pommern* still in sight, it did not take long for the racing spirit to take hold of us. Not that there was anything to be done about it except to brace round the yards quickly to every bit of breeze. For some time during the afternoon we held a narrow flaw of wind, thereby gaining a mile or two on the *Pommern*. She is a bigger ship than *L' Avenir* and is probably faster for, though she does not carry royals, her yards are very long. It must be a tough job furling her upper topgallant sails in a rising gale. A southbound Dutch steamer passed too far off for her name to be read, though a puff of wind brought the faint sound of her siren blown as a salute in passing the *Pommern*. The steamer made so many alterations of course that at first we thought she was coming to speak to us, then that she was zigzagging to avoid submarines, and finally that her helmsman was still suffering from crossing the line celebrations.

After dark and before moonrise, a light was lowered over the counter with the idea of attracting fish, but apart from a few small flying fish flitting about anxiously just below the surface, and for an occasional phosphorescent shape deep down, there was little to be seen.

To celebrate May 1st according to the Scandinavian custom, we all gathered on the poop in the moonlight to enjoy mead, and a sort of twisted sweet cheese-straw without the cheese, while the steward's boy gave us a concert on the captain's gramophone. Yet another steamer overtook us, but she was so far away that only the lights at her mastheads were visible.

The next morning to our intense satisfaction, the *Pommern* was well abaft the beam and closer. Several times we could see that her sails were flapping while ours were full. A school of about twenty bonito took station round the bows looking so eminently catchable that every owner of a fishing line who was off watch mustered on the jibboom. The donkey-man had just finished making a huge six-pronged trident which had been secured to a fifteen feet spar. When the captain arrived forward carrying this, needing only a fireman's helmet and a bicycle to impersonate Britannia, the stowaway gave a sigh of relief, for he had been told by the crew that the fearsome looking trident had been specially made as an instrument of torture for Father Neptune, when he came aboard on crossing the line.

Though the bonito flatly refused to be hooked, speared or otherwise wheedled out of the sea, they were wonderfully beautiful to watch in the clear blue water; besides various shades of green on their backs, and a flash of white from underneath as they turned, they had a patch of purple near their tails which was so vivid, that when they dived down together, the sea was patterned with shimmering purple lights which faded imperceptibly away into the blue depths.

The shout of 'Shark' aroused an excitement which must have been born of the sailors' inherent fear of these loathsome creatures. This particular one was only about seven feet long and its green-brown colour and light markings on the fins could be seen very clearly as it swam slowly round the ship. Sharks are not built for speed, nor do they look powerful in the water, but there is something very terrible about the shape of the head, even when one cannot see their small but baleful eyes.

A large hook with a heavy trace of chain was fetched quickly and dropped over the stern, baited with the traditional lump of salt pork. The mate was master fisherman and his method was to keep dragging the bait away from the shark in order to tantalize and infuriate it. This certainly had the desired effect, and eventually the shark came on in real earnest, turned over and engulfed the bait. It was struck hard, but when willing hands had hauled three-quarters of it out of water, the hook came away, and with a heavy splash it fell back into the sea. But without a moment's pause it came back at the bait. Once again it was struck, and lifted almost clear of the water, but this time as it became unhooked we could see that the side of its jaw had been badly torn. Even this was not enough to make it give up the small if tasty meal which remained, and it kept swimming close around the hook examining it closely, and sometimes touching the line with its body or tail.

As the ship was only moving slowly and the sea was crystal clear we could follow every movement of a sucker fish which accompanied the shark. Quite small, it appeared silver-blue, white or light yellow in the water, and spent most of the time half-way along the shark's back either swimming or attached behind the dorsal fin. It must be admitted that we saw no signs of the sucker fish trying to warn its host off the danger in the bait, unless it whispered advice in its ear. As far as could be seen the sucker fish took remarkably good care to remain well abaft the shark's mouth.

After a time, as the shark's appetite remained feeble, another slightly smaller shark hook, also mounted on a chain, was brought out and baited with another nice piece of pork. Immediately the shark rushed savagely at it, and in a moment was hauled kicking clear of the water. The line was snatched to a block on the spanker boom in such a way that the shark could be triced up, and lowered on deck, where it thrashed about furiously, scattering the spectators right and left. The captain then seized the line and, shouting like a Viking, rushed forward towing the struggling brute behind him over the coils of braces lying on the deck.

Then came a scene of savagery. After a blow on the nose with a capstan bar, the shark's tail was cut off, but not before it had dealt a shrewd blow or two. The body was then pitched down into the well-deck, and the lad who takes pleasure in butchering the pigs set to work with a knife, assisted by several other ghouls. The back fin was first cut off, then the backbone was hacked out and lastly, when it was presumably quite dead, the jaws were removed. A strong and ghastly smell hung over the forepart of the ship. All this was within a few minutes of its having directed nasty looks at us from the sea.

Frassie, the captain's cat, and Josephina, had not been forgotten and were down in the well-deck enjoying dainty morsels. The shark's backbone is quite whippy and to make it into a walking-stick a steel rod has to be put down the centre. Actually none of the shark family – dog fish, skate, rays, or tope – have any true bone in their skeletons, but only cartilage. This shows that they are a stage farther back in evolution than the bony fishes, than which they are less adaptable and less numerous in both kinds and numbers.

The sucker fish had been found firmly attached to the shark, but it had changed colour to black, no doubt as a last tribute of respect to its patron. It was only four inches long, its shape reminding one of a gurnard but with a strong sucker, ribbed like the sole of a gym shoe, placed underside up on the top of its head. The boys amused themselves by sticking the wretched creature on each other's bare backs and calves.

This sucker fish is the remora and is a most interesting example of adaptation, for when small, it is quite normal, having a back fin like any respectable fish. As it grows up, the back fin gradually moves forward to the top of the head, where it develops into a most efficient sucking disc.

Sucker Fish

The value of the remora has been recognized by the natives in the Caribbean sea, Torres Straits, and China seas, who secure a fine line through a hole bored in its tail, and use it for fishing and for catching turtles. It is in the Torres Straits that the latter are caught with the remora, which is thrown towards the quarry when the fisherman's canoe has got as near as possible to the turtle without disturbing it. Should a large green turtle dive, no attempt is made to lift it by means of the sucker fish, but a native dives down and secures a rope to its flipper. So far so good, but these natives can hardly be regarded as true sportsmen, for when the day's fishing is over the unhappy remora is eaten.

The shark's skin is useful on board for cleaning woodwork. It is as rough as sandpaper and has the advantage that it can be used wet. In obedience to sailing ship tradition, the shark's tail and fins were nailed fast to the extreme end of the bowsprit.

The leaden sky almost touching a sea whitened by the spray of falling water hung like a curtain close round the ship. The word downpour fails to express the almost solid torrents of rain which made the ship more like a submarine than anything else. Water cascaded down the sails on to the flooded deck, and above the noise it made could be heard the thin forlorn sound of the foghorn, its two long blasts proclaiming to anyone within earshot that we were a sailing ship on the port tack. The lookout on the forecastle head had been certain that he had heard the sound of a siren, but nothing could be seen through the water-laden air beyond a hundred yards or so.

These tropical rains can be a greater source of danger than fog, for steamships may delay reducing speed, arguing that the weather will probably clear soon and that it is unlikely that there are any other ships in the vicinity. It is an anxious time for the captain, for apart from this risk, there may come swirling out of the murk a squall of wind taking the ship aback.

Should she have insufficient way on, and the wind comes from somewhere ahead, a stern board will have to be made, during which she is vulnerable to an extra fierce puff, which will endanger the rigging.

This is no time of rest for the crew, for often the watch below may be summoned up by the three sharp whistle blasts to brace round the yards quickly. They come up with the minimum of clothing, with the rain glistening on their bare backs. When the breeze failed the watch on deck would be employed collecting the rainwater from the tubs and scuppers, and carrying the precious stuff in buckets to the galley, where it was poured down into one of the ship's tanks to form a reserve supply.

In the heave of the swell, when the rain had beaten down the wind, the old sails swung as stiff as boards, with the patches on them bulging full of water like monstrous blisters. In the intervals when there was neither wind nor rain, the sea looked and sounded like a tide race, such as one meets off Portland Bill. Though not heavy, it was very confused, small columns of water being reared up vertically then collapsing with a splash. Most likely this was caused by the meeting of the swells originated by the SE. and NE. trades.

Although they had been washed down every evening, the decks had been so warped by the tropical sun that rain poured through in several places, lodging in the alleyways, where it had to be baled out. No skylight has yet been invented which will keep out water; that above the dining saloon was no exception, for it would have been a real success as a shower bath.

Whether or no it was the result of the thousands of tons of fresh water falling into the sea during the day, there was an amazing display of phosphorescence after dark. Deep down could be seen huge luminous shapes coming to life for a moment and then fading away, while nearer the surface minute creatures would sparkle for an instant like drowning stars. When a fishing line was hauled in, it looked like an incandescent wire. The eddies under the stern stimulated great phosphorescent activity, which went swirling off into the wake; sometimes there would be brought up to the surface a sausage-shaped creature which would glow with an intensely green light.

Late in the afternoon of the eighty-seventh day smoke was seen on the horizon to windward. As masts and funnel came in sight, we realized with disappointment that the steamer would certainly pass a long way astern of us. But as soon as her bridge appeared over the rim of the sea, she altered course in our direction. British stock being low since the *Dunely* had spurned us, the captain and mates maintained that this stranger must belong to the Finnish line which trades to South America. An approaching rain squall brought a freshening breeze, but although the steamer had to alter course twice more to intercept us she came within half a mile of us before resuming her original track. Just as dusk was falling a light flashed from her bridge, and the following conversation took place:

'What ship?'

'Finnish barque *L'Avenir*.'

'I. M. I.' (Which means, 'Please repeat — I Missed It.')

'Finnish barque *L'Avenir*.'

'I. M. I.'

'*L'Avenir*. What ship?'

'British S.S. *Pencisely*.' (Cheers and 'I told you so' from us, for the captain's benefit.)

'I. M. I.'

'*Pencisely*.'

'I. M. I.'

'*Pencisely*. I will report you to Lloyd's. Good voyage.'

'Thank you. Good night.'

'Cheerio.'

It was a pity the distance prevented us from saying that we were grateful for her courtesy in coming so far out of her way, but perhaps such feelings get across without any visible Morse code.

The following evening we enjoyed a second conversation with a ship which passed within range of the flashing lamp. She signalled that she was the Dutch S.S. *Aalsum* from Rotterdam to Buenos Aires, and gave us the longitude. After we had told her our name and the number of days out from Australia, we asked, 'Any news?' Her reply: 'Same crisis all over.

Wishing you a good voyage,' caused a good deal of discussion afterwards, but it was generally decided that it meant that the depression was still ruling the world. We rather wished that we had not asked for news.

CHAPTER XX

THE LINE

AT times there is something sinister about the doldrums. They abandon themselves to extremes in a manner which shocks northern convention. One can imagine the fear creeping over a sailing ship that baffling and contrary squalls, unknown currents, and calms of molten brass, might conspire to hold her until food should run out and ropes go rotten.

For the six days we had averaged less than twenty miles a day, for even when there was a light breeze, a swell and an adverse current reduced its effect. On board there was a feeling of suspense.

Overhead the sky was blue and to the north the horizon was vividly clear with a few golden clouds hanging lightly above it. But away to the south were two huge clouds separated from each other by a narrow rift of light. These cloud masses were so purple black that it seemed as if night had rebelled against the dominion of the sun. Gradually they spread up towards the zenith.

Early in the morning a small shark had been caught and eaten for breakfast in the forecastle. Whether this was real hunger, scientific interest, bravado, or to emphasize dissatisfaction with the victuals provided, could not be discovered. Those who partook of it said that the shark was not bad eating, nor unduly fishy or oily, but somehow no one felt they wanted to eat much of it. The flesh was white. It was found that the pigs thoroughly relished raw shark.

We crossed a queer line of foam stretching as far as eye could see roughly east and west. In it were countless Portuguese men-of-war and larger jellyfish. George the stowaway was told that it was the Line, but he had got suspicious since he had heard that the patent log was no longer being used in case it might get foul of the line. Actually the accumulation of foam and jelly fish usually marks the meeting of two ocean currents and therefore it is natural to find a lot of drifting life there.

A huge ray was disturbed by the ship, while sleeping near the surface, and it flapped its way out of our path. Rays often have sucker fish living at their expense, and this may account for the fact that they are sometimes seen to leap clear into the air, falling flat on the water with a noise like a gunshot. On the south coast of Java, there are rays which are more feared than sharks by bathers, for they come into quite shallow water and give such a tearing bite that the victim rarely recovers.

Flying fish were not plentiful though sometimes a covey would be put up by some big fish, which would cause a boiling swirl, or perhaps show a flash of blue, green and white as it turned over near the surface.

Sharks seem to obey the law of the sea and to keep out of sight when the sun is high, unless of course they catch sight of a meal, when savage hunger overcomes every other instinct. Our next shark was caught at dusk with wonderful ease and efficiency, though it nearly dragged in Charlie, the steward's boy, who was wriggling about on the rail with excitement, while trying to help with the line. It is a thrilling moment when the shark is lowered on deck and thrashes about with its tail. Judging by the noise its strength must be enormous. The well-deck was again used for dismembering the shark; in the failing light with an occasional flash from an electric torch the scene might well have been a cannibal orgy. The pigs must have thought that their last hour had come, for they became very noisy, and this with the strong smell of shark added atmosphere to the awful rites.

This shark had three sucker fish, and after they had been out of water for a quarter of an hour, we put the largest into a bath of salt water. About six inches long, it revived rapidly, though it was an hour before it regained its pale blue-white colour. The most interesting feature was that it was evidently quite content to be upside down. The sucker is on top of its head, and for some time it remained stuck firmly to the bottom of the bath; even when removed to a more comfortable position on the side of the bath, it would at once return to the bottom and lie upside down. Later when it began to swim round, it did so the right way up, but would occasionally do a complete roll over as if to keep in practice for sticking on to the top of a shark's back at short notice. Immediately it was removed from the water it turned black once more.

No wonder the stowaway had been apprehensive about crossing the line. Being the only one of the crew who had not already been initiated, he would be certain to get undivided time and attention. There was no ceremony with ingeniously made robes, but only a crude effort to hand on the punishment deserved for being a greenhorn.

The noon sight had put us eleven miles north of the equator, which we must have crossed early in the morning, but it was after the day's work, and just as it was getting dusk, that George was hailed into the well-deck by half a dozen of the boys, while the remainder watched from above. After being blindfolded with a black handkerchief, the victim was dosed with a foul looking concoction of mustard and oil by Danska who, as youngest in the forecastle, was allowed to be Chief Tormentor. Then with a huge brush, he was lathered and generally bespattered with some black tarry looking stuff, on to which was stuck teased out rope yarns, to give the appearance of the healthy growth of hair cultivated by the hardy sailor. Next he was shaved with a ghastly looking knife, with a notched and pointed blade eighteen inches long. Buckets of water were flung over him and finally he was immersed head down three times running in a

[*facing:* Acrobatics on a lower topgallant yard-
George the stowaway is the right-hand fi

cask of brine, which had been the home of salt horse, into which his shoulders would only just fit. As everyone knew that his wardrobe was not extensive, George had been allowed to shed his trousers before the lathering began. All the time he remained perfectly cheerful and did not show the slightest sign of resentment, which was just as well, for any hint of rebellion would have been squashed by the forecastle en bloc.

On this day we were about fifty miles west of St. Paul Rocks so that it was presumably from them that there arrived a couple of butterflies, one with orange wings with black edges spotted with white, the other black and white, and also a dragon fly.

Though why butterflies should live on St. Paul Rocks is difficult to understand, for they are only a few hundred yards in extent and the highest is only sixty-four feet above the sea. The rocks are volcanic and are covered with guano. In the past ships have often reported that they have struck rocks or banks near the equator, from the St. Paul Rocks to the eastward, but it is now known that an earthquake at sea produces an exactly similar feeling, and that all this area is subject to volcanic disturbances.

The day following the crossing of the line made us unsettled and annoyed. Conveniently after breakfast, a ship was sighted steering straight for us, evidently homeward bound. As we were wallowing about in a long swell under a blazing sun with hardly any breeze, the thought that she was sure to come close and give us some news was definitely refreshing. As she approached and altered course slightly, to pass under our stern, we saw that she was a motor cargo ship of a type which carries about a dozen passengers. There is not much more to add.

The ship was the M.S. *Brittany* of Liverpool and she honk-a-tonked past at full speed, just outside hailing distance, without even hoisting her colours. We could see the nice cool-looking swimming tank built on the fore well-deck, and we watched the passengers and white-clad officers so busy taking 'happy snaps' with their little Kodaks that none of them bothered to wave. But then they were not even interested enough to inquire how many days out we were. Of course Finland is a small country and a sailing ship has not many people on board, but even the smallest gesture of friendliness from the *Brittany* would have given much pleasure and would have been talked about for days.

After spending a fortnight in them people were really beginning to wonder if we were ever going to shake ourselves clear of the moist tentacles of the doldrums.

The inside of the ship became very hot, for of course there were no fans, and often the dining saloon skylight had to be kept closed because of the rain. All the scuttles (or portholes) must be kept permanently closed when the ship is fully loaded, for a strong squall of wind would easily force the ship to lie over until the lee ones were under water; this would be highly dangerous as it is difficult to get water out of a sailing ship.

Unhappily for our progress, the squalls contained more water than wind. Often a black cloud would sit down on the water, with quite clear-cut vertical edges of lighter cloud showing against the blue sky. They brought to mind one of the pictures in Struwel-Peter of the squall which was the undoing of Flying Robert.

At least we had no anxiety about fresh water. Ships have often been forced to rely on rainwater, and we were told that the training ship *Favell*, a small three-masted barque belonging to Helsingfors, usually spends her time in the tropics chasing showers of rain. Being old and slow she usually returns by the Cape of Good Hope, almost always taking over one hundred and forty days from Australia to Europe and sometimes as much as two hundred and ten days. Having only small tanks, water almost invariably runs short.

A few years ago when another sailing ship was in the doldrums, the chief mate, who is responsible for the fresh water, noticed that the consumption suddenly went up to five times the normal allowance. At first he naturally thought that a mistake had been made in sounding the tanks, but for the next two days the same thing occurred. Suspicion fell on the steward, and the mate suggested to the captain that he should muster the provisions. It was then found that only enough of the latter remained for fourteen days, while the voyage was expected to last at least double that. It seemed that the steward had resold some of the stores before the ship left port, and had also been retailing extra food to the crew. When he discovered that the provisions would not last out for the voyage, he began pumping fresh water overboard at night, hoping that it would be put down to a leak in the tank, and that it would make the captain go into the nearest port where food also could be obtained. Though our captain was spared these particular anxieties, he became more and more worried about our very slow progress. Also from the number of ships sighted and from the fact that the main steamer track passes to the east of St. Paul Rocks, while our sights put us to the west, he came to the conclusion that our chronometers were about four minutes wrong. Some weeks earlier wireless time signals had sometimes shown an error, but this had been put down to the casual methods of certain South American broadcasting stations. The real trouble was that faith in the chronometers had been shattered since they had been sent to be cleaned in Bristol the previous year, for within a few months after this, two out of the three had stopped as a result of wrong oil being applied.

CHAPTER XXI

NORTH-EAST TRADES

THOUGH for some time we doubted their genuineness, the NE. trades were at last born out of one of the most wretched days imaginable. Drab curtains of cloud hung around the ship without a break, the only change being when they became yet more sombre, and when the rain came down in cataracts instead of the usual torrents. Between decks it was so dark that one could barely read. The moist heat would raise a culture of mildew on any leather almost as fast as one could wipe it off. Except that the odour of scent and powder was absent, the inside of the ship was reminiscent of the Paris Metro. But as a consolation there was some breeze in spite of the rain: it was NE. to begin with, then south for a time before coming back to NNE., when the clouds began to thin out and scatter, and even the worst pessimists admitted that we might perhaps have reached the trades.

Near the equator, instead of being true NE., these trades are more northerly, becoming gradually more easterly as one goes north. Our track should therefore be a curve as we shall remain close hauled all the time, following the wind round so that we do not go any farther west than is necessary. This sailing by the wind means that, unless anything extraordinary happens, the sails should not require trimming or touching for the next thousand miles.

As soon as it was certain that the ship was well and truly in the trades, all the hands were put on to day work, except two in each watch, who took alternate hours as helmsman and lookout during the time they were on deck. Jackie and another apprentice were in one watch, Adenoid Albert and Dirty Peter in the other. While leading this extra strenuous life, Jackie spent a good deal of her time off watch curled up on a rug on one of the hatches, with a big alarm clock propped close by her head.

No more steamers should be sighted until we reach the track between Europe and the West Indies and Panama, and as we shall cross that more or less at right angles the chances are that we shall not meet anything. Since the SE. trades we have sighted about twenty steamers and have spoken three, one British, one French and one Dutch. These numbers are considered to be well above the average.

It was a delightful feeling when the ship became actively alive once more, when she began to heel over to the breeze and started off the bow wave muttering. For a long time the Great Bear had been in sight with its pointers looking down below the northern horizon. Except perhaps to the Antipodeans, it was a thrilling moment when first the Pole Star was sighted. The poor Southern Cross suffers badly by comparison with the Great Bear, but it must be remembered that as there are not many stars of first magnitude visible from Australia, the Southern Cross is much more valuable than its size merits.

The NE. trades freshened gradually, until, after a couple of days, we were doing eight knots close-hauled. The breeze had that perfect quality of feeling cool, but never making one cold even at night. It hummed and purred through the rigging, sent little bursts of spray over the forecastle head, and kept miniature rainbows playing around the bow wave. It must be like a taste of paradise to a sailing ship captain to have all his anxiety removed for about a week; to know the wind will hold true, with little variation in strength, and that even rain is unlikely.

All the sea-birds had forsaken us since just north of the line, but their place had been taken by flying-fish. Perhaps the albatross and petrel family have found it utterly impossible to catch flying-fish, which may per-haps have put their beaks out of joint to such an extent that they have crossed tropics off their visiting lists. Flying-fish had not been plentiful south of the line; probably they migrate north with the sun to a certain extent. Unless being chased, they do not seem to fly when the breeze is light. More flying was done on our leeside than on the weather one; perhaps this was due to the unexpected leeway we made upsetting their calculations.

In the NE. trades great shoals would come out of the

water together, flashing over the blue sea like showers of silver arrows and then splashing into the water as if a handful of stones had been flung after them.

The flying-fish is something like a herring in size and shape, its wings being simply greatly enlarged pectoral fins. The lower lobe of its tail is larger than the upper one. When first it comes out of the water, its wings can usually be seen to be moving for a moment, but while it is in flight the wings appear to be motionless, unless they are vibrating too fast for the eye to follow. To fly off, the fish jumps almost clear of the sea, spreads its wings and gathers speed by sculling with its tail in the water until it is going fast enough to fly. It never rises more than a few inches above the wave crests and yet sometimes brings off a flight of several hundred yards, though more often it pitches into the sea for a moment and then takes off again, when on a long flight.

During the good weather period there was a great orgy of painting all over the ship, inside and out. One of the boys had a narrow escape while standing on the main royal yard (the highest of all) painting the mast. His feet slipped on a patch of white zinc and tallow, which had been used on the standing rigging, and he fell down clear of the yard, only just managing to catch hold of the wire clewline, which runs along horizontally beneath the yard.

The trades brought with them a germ of restlessness born of the feeling that the voyage was approaching its end. Though a hundred days out and with a strong probability of the passage lasting at least another month, one became obsessed with the idea that there would not be time to complete the various projects on hand. Even packing was mentioned now and then. Plans for the future were discussed and a year-old copy of the London daily *Times* was dug out, and re-read over and over again with real pleasure. There is an unlimited amount of raw material in the *Times* for the building of a dream life, and even the financial pages are not really depressing, owing to the possibility that some apparently dead investment may have blossomed unaccountably in the meantime. But the pleasantest occupation was the selecting of luxurious suites (with bath-room) in London hotels, conveniently close to theatres and shops, and in choosing Desirable Gentlemen's Residences in park-like surroundings and staffing them with Superior Well-trained Servants. It was about this time that letter-writing began in earnest, as it was quite certain that none would get written within a month or so of arriving.

The dining saloon was painted out, and for a few days we migrated forward to a compartment which had been part of the schoolroom in training ship days. There was a square window looking out on to the well-deck which made the water sound extremely close as it swished in through the freeing ports: the grunting of the pigs supplied a 'truly rural' touch.

As the voyage progressed, the presence of rats on board became more and more evident. When she arrived in Australia, *L'Avenir* had been fumigated in accordance with the regulations, but the efficacy of this is doubtful, considering the small number of dead rats found afterwards.

It was during the cold weather in the southern ocean that the rats first began to be a nuisance, for they used to raid the galley every night. Not for food, for with over three thousand tons of wheat on board, they had no difficulty about that, but to get material for their nests. Any clothes left there overnight to dry were liable to have pieces eaten out of them; one almost new leather coat was ruined in this way. It was this habit of the rats which saved the temper of the cook from being permanently soured, for his galley had been so inundated with wet clothes that it was becoming increasingly impossible to get near the range.

In the warm weather, for some reason unknown, unless it was an urge for pure seamanship, a rat would sometimes go aloft, not by the ordinary shrouds, but up the braces. It was easy enough to shake him off into the sea, unless Josephina the cat happened to be near. She was wonderful with rats and was not afraid of even the largest and fiercest father of a family. Even before her kitten came off milk diet, Josephina would often be seen looking for it during the evening, emitting muffled mews, due to having a struggling rat in her mouth. She reminded one of a parent returning home from the City with a rather unwieldy toy for the young hopeful.

Towards the end of the voyage, the rats began to get above themselves. One evening, the steward's boy, the smallest person on board, was sitting reading when a rat ran up inside his trouser leg. Charlie (all steward boys answer to this) grabbed the wriggling bulge when it was above his knee, managed to crush the rat to death without getting bitten and then slipped out of his trousers as if they had caught fire.

Whenever the holds were opened for ventilation, one could see at a glance the sort of damage that rats do to a cargo. Although there was no lack of wheat lying about, they had seemed to take pleasure in ripping open fresh bags.

We were unable to discover whether the rats obtained any fresh water, or whether they could get on without. Another problem remained unsolved; if eight rabbits consume as much pasture as one sheep, how many rats would it take to eat a human's ration?

CHAPTER XXII

NEAR THE TROPIC OF CANCER

THOUGH they may be called inanimate objects, sails sometimes display the cussedness of humans. The mizen royal chose Sunday afternoon to split down the middle, with no provocation whatever beyond a nice fresh trade wind. It was an old sail, a relic of the Belgian days and having a coat-of-arms on it, the paint had burnt the canvas in the centre so that there it was quite rotten although the rest of the sail was serviceable.

As there were still only two men in each watch, it was decided not to turn out the remainder of the hands, but to shift the sail with the second and third mates up aloft supported by George the stowaway and three passengers. The captain took the wheel while the chief mate, the sailmaker and his mates, and Jackie worked on deck. When the time came to send up the fresh sail, they were assisted on the gantline by the steward, cook, and a couple of boys who happened to be about. Though it was most irregular, the hands aloft gave them a hauling shanty. Even in the old days, the Scandinavians had no shanties of their own, but used the English or American ones. Nowadays with young crews, none are ever used in

[*facing:* In the Tropics. Bending on an old

practice, though one often hears 'Shenandoah' or 'We are off to the Rio Grande' whistled or sung about the ship.

It was especially interesting to watch George at work aloft after only three months on board this or any ship, most of which had been spent in chipping, scraping, cleaning out the pigsty, and doing anything but seamanship. In spite of having started several years too late, though not very quick at doing anything out of the ordinary, he is really useful aloft. It is pathetic that so much good material must be going to waste through unemployment, and that, as likely as not, when the voyage is over, George himself may be forced to tramp the English roads with the hope of getting a man's job ebbing slowly away.

Whit-Monday was a general holiday, and in the forecastle it was spent in playing poker for cigarettes. One of the remarkable features of a long voyage is that money gradually loses its significance. Nobody carries any about with them, and there is nothing to buy, except soap, cigarettes and matches, for which the captain gives credit. It is only by coming across attractive advertisements in illustrated papers that £ s. d. comes into one's mind at all. No wonder that the sailors of the beginning of the last century and before were so childish about money. In time of war, when prizes were plentiful, a prime seaman might easily be paid off from a warship with a couple of hundred pounds. By the time they reached London, a large proportion of the men who left ships, even at Chatham, had lost everything to the hosts of land sharks of all sorts, whose business it was to relieve them of all anxiety about worldly possessions. This reckless spending was not quite so stupid as it sounds, for a good seaman might consider himself lucky if he escaped the press-gang for more than a few days after leaving his last ship. It is difficult to realize the heartlessness of those days when at the end of a long voyage, a merchantship might receive a visit from the press-gang, which would take as many of her crew as were needed to some man-of-war, in which they might have to serve for years, before getting back to their homes.

In about 20° N. the trades began to get fickle. Instead of the usual fleecy clouds, black rain squalls made their appearance from time to time; short calms of a quarter of an hour were followed by fresh breezes, which would make the ship lie right over and tear through the water. Happily the wind remained true in direction, not much north of east. The captain had planned to go north between the longtitudes of 40° and 45° W., as here the horse latitudes are narrower and when once through them there is a chance of picking up strong westerlies.

Perhaps it was the complete absence of sea-birds during the preivous few days that had made the ocean seem rather more lonely than usual. Or it may be we had been spoiled by the amount of traffic seen in the doldrums. Most of the world's shipping keeps to definite tracks, so that there must be huge areas where one might drift for years without sighting anything. For the North Atlantic, there is a shipping agreement in which separate outward and homeward tracks are laid down like tramlines, so that fast mail liners can tear their way through hazy weather with a little less anxiety. Some distance to the south-east of Newfoundland these tracks change direction quite sharply, but as there is no policeman on point duty, some captains must find it very difficult to resist the temptation to cut the corners.

A grizzly ceremony took place in the well-deck. A small bonfire was lit, the boys brought their beds out of the forecastle and held them over the fire until the material just began to scorch, when the bugs dropped out into the flames. These pests get into the woodwork of a ship so that it is almost impossible to get rid of them altogether. Fortunately there were no Minor Horrors in the cabins.

On the one hundred and sixth day at noon, if we had been seven miles farther south the sun would have been exactly overhead. As it was, one could bring the sun down to the horizon with a sextant, spin round on one's heel, and still keep the sun in the field of view of the telescope.

Just to the southward of the Tropic of Cancer we came across the first pieces of sargassum weed, floating just below the surface. On the forecastle George said, 'what would you like? whelks, crabs or lobsters? Someone had made a ring net and was fishing up sprays of weed a foot in diameter. Among it were found crabs the size of a thumbnail, minute shell-fish, prawns an eighth of an inch long and the eggs of some sort of fish.

The weed is a yellow-brown colour which shows up vividly against the intensely blue sea. It grows on a stem which looks as if it had broken off a larger branch. The weed itself is quite delicate with light brown berry-like bladders. The stalks become browner towards the main branch, which is dark. This floating weed has no organs of reproduction. It is supposed that growing weed has been torn off the coasts of central America and the West Indies, and has been carried into, and kept in, this huge slow Atlantic whirl by the currents which flow round it.

On the one hundred and ninth day began a calm which was almost uncanny. Sea and cloudless sky of steel merged together with only a faint line between them. Not the softest breeze furrowed the surface of the sea and only a slight swell sent the dark shadow-lines chasing each other lazily over the burnished face of the waters. The sails hung sagging and lifeless, and only the occasional creak of the complaining sheave of some block, a voice, or perhaps a laugh, would break the silence. The sun beat down mercilessly from almost overhead, bringing the pitch welling out of the deck seams in shining bubbles.

Looking straight downwards close alongside the ship, the sea was of the most heavenly turquoise blue. From the shadow of one's head radiated out beams of twisting light, so that sinners as well as saints could get some idea of how they would look in halos. The patches of sargassum weed were becoming more frequent; from some of the larger pieces, the upper fronds would protrude above the surface. The sea itself looked as if the carpenter had been emptying mahogany sawdust into it from the masthead, but quite suddenly towards noon, except for a few shining specks it became clear.

Two large tins which had been thrown overboard early in the day remained in sight for hours, breaking the magic circle of the horizon. Near by a cruising fish would sometimes furrow or ring the surface, while deep down by the turn of the bilge, other fish would sometimes dart out for a moment from their shelter in the shadow of the hull.

Except that a potato crisis was approaching, and the cheese contained a school of unnecessarily athletic grubs, we had no cause to worry. But it was now easier to understand the fear which must have laid its cold hand on the ignorant sailors of olden times, when they met a deadly and hopeless calm with the weed appearing to collect round them, and to clutch at the rough, barnacle-coated hull of their ship.

Some of the crew were positive that they had seen some sea-snakes about six inches to a foot long, but their accounts varied to such an extent that it was impossible to confirm their stories, or identify the species. There are sea-snakes which are highly poisonous, and have developed flattened tails and keeled bodies to improve their swimming powers; but these live in tropic seas where shelter is easier to obtain than in the open ocean.

Land snakes are liable to be met in unexpected places. On one occasion a party landed on an island inside the Great Barrier Reef, between twenty and thirty miles off the coast of Queensland, to shoot the succulent Cape York pigeon which come over from the mainland every evening to roost. The island was typical of the region, consisting of a narrow circle of broken coral, only a few feet above the high water mark, enclosing a shallow lagoon. Coarse grass, shrubs and mangrove trees grow in profusion wherever they can find root. It was among the long grass that one of the party, wearing shorts and no stockings, trod on a seven-foot brown snake of a highly poisonous variety. The most probable explanation was that it had been washed down one of the Queensland rivers in a tree, which had eventually drifted near the island. Anyhow, the snake was shot and is now back on the continent as a pair of shoes.

Towards the late afternoon, the sawdust effect was again noticed in the sea; in some places it formed into a brown scum. There were also small jelly-fish which looked exactly like smoke rings.

After having been deserted by birds for some days, more storm petrels came in sight. They were rather shy at first but eventually came close enough to be identified as Leach's storm petrels. They have longer wings than our old friends the Wilson's variety, and evidently have nasty mocking natures, to call themselves storm petrels and then come hovering round us in the flattest calm imaginable.

The sunset was so lovely that even the captain's gloom was dispelled for a time. The few scattered clouds and the whole undulating surface of the sea were pink. Between the depth of the sky and the horizon was a band of grey. The watching moon and the still clouds were mirrored in the water. As the sun sank in a blaze of fiery orange, it seemed as if it was pouring out molten metal, which spread over the face of the sea as it came towards us.

A moment after the sun had completely disappeared, we had a perfect view of the green flash. It was as if the sun had obtruded a wide green flame some twentieth of its diameter in height and width. The word flash hardly expresses the phenomenon accurately, because it was visible for nearly two seconds. The moment it disappeared, one of the interested observers dashed aloft as quickly as possible, but even then failed to be the first person to see the green flash twice in one day.

As the bright colours in the west were fading out very slowly, to the east sea and sky merged together.

Gradually the clouds showed whiter against the darkening sky, until at last our whole world lay under the sway of the moon's aloof majesty. But hours later as midnight was approaching, she became almost skittish, for as we lay on top of one of the hatches, she played hide and seek with us in and out among the black sails. *L'Avenir* became a fairy ship with the moonlight reflecting off the new white paint; every rope could be seen outlined against the sky.

For a time we thought that the Leprecaun had become either moonstruck or else unhinged by the calm, for we noticed him behaving in an extremely queer way, progressing backwards on hands and knees along the teak rail which runs round the outside of the ship, measuring it with a two-foot rule. It was not until the following day that we discovered he was only satisfying a passion for computation by 'heaving a Dutch log'. If a floating object is thrown overboard from somewhere forward, and the time is taken for it to reach some position aft, the speed of the ship can be worked out. Instead of pacing out the distance required in a manner which would have satisfied mere human accuracy, the Leprecaun felt urged to get it correct to a fraction of an ell. Having got this right, he flung a chip of wood overboard forward. But before it quite reached the after observation post, it changed direction and drifted out of sight ahead. A bright lookout was kept and some half-hour later, the piece of wood reappeared and at last got past the post. After profound calculations, the Leprecaun discovered that we were making ·001 knots.

The following morning was calmer still, if possible, though the clear break between deep blue sea and light blue sky, with some cotton-wool clouds, gave the hope of a breeze. It was remarkable that though the sea was glassy, except for a slight and long northerly swell, even though the ship sometimes seemed to be stopped dead, she never quite lost steerage way. During the calm when the *Pommern* was in sight, we had noticed her pointing all round the compass while we remained heading on our course.

Calm usually begins arguments about the value of auxiliary engines for sailing ships. The captain says that the German auxiliary four-masted barque *Magdelene Vinnen* never makes a good passage, for the drag of the propeller prevents her from ever doing more than about eight knots, even with the most favourable gale. The smaller Baltic coasting ships also find the same thing, that a propeller prevents them from sailing fast. For a deep-water sailing ship, besides the obvious disadvantages of cost of installation and fuel, there is the expense of at least two engineers, the loss of cargo space, and the fact that no auxiliary engine is powerful enough to enable a sailing ship to be handled safely in a harbour, in anything but a very moderate breeze.

The promise of morning was kept, for at noon a light breeze arrived, dead ahead to begin with but freeing as the day went on. At this stage of the voyage a calm is most undesirable, for although most of those on board are in no real hurry to arrive, it causes tempers to become short and makes them liable to flare up, so that any chance remark may end in a fight. Sunday is always the worst day for a calm, because then everyone is conscious of the waste of time. During the week, while the hands are working, the ship's progress is more of an incident to be noted and dismissed from the mind.

Opinion in the forecastle usually blames the captain, quite unjustly, for a bad passage; though of course loyalty to the ship would make them die rather than admit it to any outsider. The German boys say that their ships carry special secret charts supplied by the German naval authorities which enable them alone to keep in perpetually strong winds. That the German ships *Priwall* and *Padua* do make consistently fast passages cannot be denied, but besides being fairly new, they carry large crews, so that no time is wasted when bracing round the yards to each puff of wind. Their captains are renowned for holding on to sail until the last possible moment.

CHAPTER XXIII

SARGASSO SEA, STEAMERS, FISH

TOWARDS the evening on the one hundred and thirteenth day there was a cheerful shout, 'Steamer in sight!' She was to the westward, and coming in our direction. Before long it was easy to see that she was a large oil-tanker, and from her track it seemed fairly certain that she must be bringing oil from the Californian oilfields, via the Panama Canal, to the Mediterranean. For a time she altered course or else yawed towards us, but then she appeared to decide quite wrongly that we were sailing too fast, as she resumed her original course. This took her some three miles astern of us, not quite near enough to distinguish her name, but close enough to see that she was Norwegian. She dipped her ensign to us, a courtesy to which we replied at once.

Some of these Norwegian tankers have never been back to Norway since first they were built. The crews sign on for a year at a time, and can miss a voyage whenever they can afford it, and care to take the risk of not getting another job when they want one. The captain may occasionally get a year's holiday while the chief mate takes command, or the owners may perhaps allow him to have his wife and family on board for a voyage or two.

Nearly everyone on board remained on deck, following the tanker with their eyes, until she disappeared into the dusk to the eastward, leaving minds freed for the moment from the thrall of routine and hard work to look into the future, with its uncertainties, hopes, fears and disappointments. To some of us these days will be remembered as unbelievably perfect, while to others they may remain a nightmare.

On the way to Australia one of the crew fell sick, and to his utter grief, the hospital to which he was sent on arrival, pronounced that he had T.B. fairly badly. Owing to the risk of infection, it was with reluctance that the captain allowed him to return in the ship. Having completed his required service in sailing ships his next step would have been to a navigation school to pass for his mate's ticket. But now, with the shattering of his dreams, the voyage will seem to him not only as a complete waste of time and energy, but as the frayed end of a life of full activity.

Towards 27° N. there was a definite change in the appearance of the sargassum weed, for a great number of the berries had come off the plants and were floating separately, or had formed a sort of scum. The weed itself was also becoming more common and was ranged in parallel lines lying north-east and south-west. Sometimes we passed small islands of it, though these were rare, and we never saw one large enough to cause apprehension to even the most under-canvassed yacht.

It is possible that the Sargasso Sea may have been discovered first of all by the ancient Phoenicians, for they gave accounts of quantities of seaweed floating in the open ocean. But like some modern navigators, the Phoenicians made a mystery of their art, and kept their routes a secret, so that few records and no maps have been preserved which throw light on their voyages.

It is a surprising fact that the Sargasso Sea is extremely poor in plankton; it is thought to be as barren as any region in the world.

The creatures found amongst the weed showed the most wonderful examples of protective colouring, causing great interest on the forecastle, where all the amateur naturalists off watch would be poring over buckets and tins. There was a queer little jelly-fish which, when shaken out of the weed, lay on the deck in a shapeless quivering mass, but when restored to water, looked rather like a child's headless stuffed animal, but was of a most delicate brown colour with frilled edges. A three-inch long fish of extraordinary and rather forbidding appearance was found among the weed. It was brown and yellow mottled; its pectoral fins began like arms and ended in fans which had eight spines, fingers or toes projecting from them, on which it appeared to walk. On its head were two nodding plumes something like feather dusters, which gave it the dignity of a Korean gentleman in national dress.

About this time we must have been crossing the eel track. It was only in 1922 that Dr. Schmidt, a famous Danish oceanographer, solved the Great Eel Mystery. Until then no one knew exactly how the eels of European rivers multiplied, as their eggs and tiny young had never been identified. It was known that in the late summer and autumn, when about a foot or more long, and from five to twenty years old, eels put on the silver 'spawning livery' and went down to the sea: and that every year countless little 'elvers', typical eels a few inches long, ascended the rivers where they fed and grew.

Dr. Schmidt discovered that the European eels make an amazing journey of two or three thousand miles in order to spawn in the Sargasso Sea. These silver eels have never actually been seen there, in fact they are lost to observation directly they reach deep water, but by marking eels in the Baltic which have been recaptured in the North Sea, it has been shown that they have travelled nine miles a day for some three months.

At the end of the winter and at the beginning of spring, the baby eels appear in the Sargasso Sea, looking utterly unlike their parents, for they are flattened sideways to leaf shape and are quite transparent. They set off for Europe and growing in size, but reducing in numbers, they take about three years over the journey. When near the coasts, they are about three inches long, and it is then that the remarkable transition to eel shape takes place.

No doubt it is their transparence which allows any of them to survive. This recalls a bright invention submitted to the Admiralty during the war, which was designed to combat the submarine menace. Fast motor boats were to be made entirely of glass, so that they would be quite invisible to their helpless prey. Presumably the crew would have had to wear cellophane clothing, unless Gieves, the naval outfitters, had been able to provide boat cloaks of invisibility.

From time to time we had a short visit from one or two red billed tropic birds, known as boatswain birds by sailors as they have long thin tails which resemble marline spikes. They are lovely birds, white except for a couple of black crescent-shaped bars on each wing, and a heavy orange or coral-red beak. The two central tail feathers are enormously elongated and trail behind the bird most gracefully, following in a curve like the wake of a ship as it alters course. They have long wings and fly with strong rapid beats recalling the flight of the pigeon; they only soar occasionally, and then but for a moment, and one has the impression that they must soon settle on board for a rest. Those that we saw flew most of the time at or above the height of the masthead. When they sight any food – fish or squid are their usual diet — they fly down towards it and then plunge the last fifty feet.

As a rule they do not remain on the water for long, and while on it, the tail is elevated.

In 27° N. we received a visit from a single great skua. This was unexpected as by rights it ought to have been well to the north for the breeding season. It was a large dark brown bird with wide wings, re-calling those of a buzzard but with a white bar on them. It had a rather heavy flight and for half an hour it circled the ship, now and then settling in the wake for a short time.

Skuas can be called sea birds of prey, for though they will feed on carrion or on any floating animal refuse, they prefer bullying gulls, terns and shear-waters out of their food. The skua attacks them until they drop whatever they have caught, and if high enough up the skua will nose dive on to it before it reaches the sea.

Opportunity of the fine weather was taken to paint out the forecastle. The weather was important as the occupants had to sleep out on deck. The bunks are in double tiers and are made of iron. It was a horrid sight when they were brought out into the well-deck, for the corners underneath all the angle irons were literally alive with obscene-looking bugs. When once these pests get well settled into a compartment, it is almost impossible to get rid of them except by tearing out every bit of wood.

The forecastle is a fair size, and besides a table and stools it contains good lockers for the stowage of clothes. It is lit by hanging oil lamps. While the painting was in progress the table and stools were kept in the well-deck, and the boys had their meals out there. The mates never go inside the forecastle, the cleanliness of which is considered to be entirely the business of the occupants. One of the watch on deck is, however, allowed time after each meal to wash up, and to do some cleaning.

Birds are queer creatures and have characters quite as various as humans. Some are fatally curious while others, even though sociably inclined, are painfully aloof. An example of this latter attitude was given towards evening while we were lying becalmed. For about half an hour there was a minor migration of a few dozen petrels in groups or singly. They were making towards the east in a purposeful way. It is a never failing source of wonder how birds of the ocean know when to make these definite movements in pursuit of food. Although they may be a thousand or more miles from any land they will keep direction with an air of complete confidence. Our ship happened to be lying in their path so they altered course to pass a mile under her stern, just far enough to prevent one from identifying them with certainty. Probably they were greater shearwaters. Our feelings were somewhat similar to those of the people on board Anson's ship, the *Centurion*, when she arrived off Macao in 1742, and at dawn found herself surrounded by a swarm of Chinese fishing junks or sampans . . .

'But what surprised us most was the inattention and want of curiosity which we observed in this herd of fishermen. A ship like ours had doubtless never been in these seas before; and perhaps there might not be one amongst all the Chinese, employed in that fishery, who had ever seen any European vessel; so that we might reasonably have expected to have been considered by them as a very uncommon and extraordinary object. But though many of their boats came close to the ship, yet they did not appear to be at all interested in us, nor did they deviate in the least from their course to regard us, which insensibility, especially of maritime persons, in a matter relating to their own profession, is scarcely to be credited, did not the general behaviour of the Chinese in other instances furnish us with continual proofs of a similar turn of mind.'

For a time we acquired a tame albacore, at least one remained with us for a couple of days, in spite of some slight unpleasantness at the start of our comradeship. Weighing perhaps four or five pounds, it was a beautiful fish, with a blue-green back which changed colour according to the light and to its depth below the surface. But most lovely were its pectoral fins, which ended in green of such lustre that they might have been made of jade illuminated from within.

The lobes of its tail were long to the point of exaggeration, and most of the time the upper one just broke the surface. But it was so completely calm that, even when swimming well below the surface, it left a wake of spreading ripples which could be seen a hundred yards away.

The albacore preferred the bows and this was nearly its undoing, for Dirty Peter and Adenoid Albert spent their watch below in fishing for it with pieces of rag on hooks, danced about on the surface of the water to represent distressed flying-fish. This would cause the albacore to dash about in great excitement as long as the rags were kept on the move, and eventually it fell a victim to Adenoid Albert's lure. As he hauled it up, it remained still for a few seconds like a glistening streak of mother-of-pearl until it was nearly up to the bowsprit net, when it gave a kick, fell back with a splash and disappeared like a streak of lightning. Not for long, however, for after a few minutes it reappeared to continue its solemn escort almost as if nothing had happened. But its mouth was sadly injured, and it studiously avoided any more baits which were set before it.

Some of the boys said they had seen albacore take a running jump at a spray of sargassum weed, and then clean up the small fish that had been flushed out of it. While looking downwards into the sea, a large shark was seen very deep down under the stern. It is quite possible that sharks do follow ships of moderate speed for considerable distances without ever being sighted.

On one occasion while a cruiser of the Royal Australian navy was steaming from Sydney to Tasmania at twelve knots, opportunity was taken to drop a depth charge for exercise. These charges were the main weapon against submarines, as they were set to explode at a desired depth. The charge was dropped from right aft, and immediately the shock of the detonation was felt, the triangular fin of a huge shark broke surface close under the stern, and a long shining brown back was seen for a moment before the monster rolled over and disappeared. Its presence at that moment may have been a coincidence, but it is more logical to suppose that the shark had been following the ship for some time, keeping well out of sight. Except in shoal water, or when they are actually feeding on floating matter, sharks do not often show their dorsal fins clear of the water.

Besides causing the usual interest and mild excitement, the next steamer to be sighted removed a certain amount of anxiety from the captain's mind. For as has already been mentioned, the accuracy of the chronometers had been doubted, as the result of conflicting wireless time signals, and from the longitude signalled from a Dutch steamer. Since the H.T. battery for the only wireless set had expired, there was now no chance of getting the B.B.C. time signal which is one of the most powerful and easy to read. Directly it was certain that the steamer was coming our way and had altered course to pass reasonably close, the signal flags were got on deck and later the signal was hoisted asking for the longitude. The reply was, '50° 16 minutes. Bon voyage'. She was a small white French steamer evidently bound for the Mediterranean, but she passed just too far off for her name to be read.

As she fussed away into the distance, leaving a smudge of smoke hanging low over the water, her wake stirred up more than the usual number of desires and restless feelings. What has been happening in England? Has the National Government made the best use of its unique possibilities, or is it beyond the powers of human brain and of goodwill to reduce unemployment, and to ease the misery of poverty which haunts such a high percentage of the people? Has the noble cause of Disarmament made real progress, or do we continue to set a practical example which no one follows, and which only convinces the rest of the world that the star of British supremacy is waning faster than ever? Is there any hope or help being given to English agriculture, or must it be sacrificed to doubtful foreign friendships? Are enough of those people entering the lists who have the ability as well as the courage to become leaders, or do our schools continue to produce a type whose aim is to make money quickly, without too much work, in order to 'have a good time'?

One could almost hear the cries of horror from the ghosts of the clipper ship captains of old when, after a good scrubbing, our decks were painted with a thick coating of linseed oil and turpentine. It was fortunate that the ship was upright, and that the breeze remained steady for some twelve hours, because the decks were so slippery that anyone trying to walk over the worst places looked as if they had put on skates for the first time. Hauling the braces would have been quite impossible. The decks are treated in this way once a year, and though one regrets snow-white decks, as the crew of a modern sailing ship is not large enough to maintain them in that state, it is obviously better to keep the wood a uniform colour, and preserve it at the same time.

One old sailing ship captain, a well-known character, when in command of *Killoran*, used to have her poop holystoned white. One day, finding nailmarks in the sacred deck, he flew into a rage and accused the mates of having nails in their boots, and insisted on looking at them. Finding them guiltless, he got angrier still and ordered all the crew aft to have their footgear inspected. Finding only rubber or rope soles, the mate suggested that as everyone else had submitted, perhaps they had better look at the captain's boots. After some spluttering he lifted one up and sure enough they found wicked great hobnails. The old man was more furious than ever and before disappearing below for the next couple of days he shouted, 'Damned lime juicer boots, I'll never buy any more of their stuff.' And to this day he has never bought British.

A fisherman's green glass ball floating by gave a sudden reminder of home waters, and also of war time, when eyes were focused on anything small in the sea while on the lookout for periscopes. These glass floats were then used to support the top of nets made of thin wire with a huge mesh, which were shot across the probable track of submarines with the idea of fouling them. At the end of each long section of net was a large buoy which was watched by patrol craft. If the buoy began to move through the water, the whole area was depth-charged freely. Sometimes mines were secured at intervals along the nets, which would explode when bumped, and could also be fired electrically by the watching vessel.

The peace time use of these glass floats is to support the upper edge of a trawl net, while it is being towed along the bottom. The sides of the net are kept apart by otter boards which act on the principle of kites, and at the foot between the otter boards there is a long rope which drags along the sea floor and frightens the fish up until they find net above them, for the head rope is shorter than the foot rope, so that the top of the net overhangs.

In the more old-fashioned beam trawl still used by Brixham and Plymouth sailing trawlers, the wooden beam takes the place of the head rope and otter boards, being kept up by heavy iron skids at each end which slide over the bottom, and between which the foot rope sags.

As the nearest trawling ground was off the coast of Morocco, this particular float must have been drifted by the Canary current into the north equatorial current, and may perhaps have made many journeys round and round the Sargasso Sea.

Another albacore spent a few hectic hours swimming round the fore foot. Besides its slender and graceful lines its main beauty lay in the changing colours of its pectoral fins which seemed to emit a blue or blue-green light which was almost dazzling. But as hunger overcame all other feelings, the watch below brought up their fishing lines.

It was, however, an unlucky day. The fish was hooked and very nearly landed. Then as it again resumed its patrol, passing right under the stem, the captain's trident was borrowed. Two shots narrowly missed it, and each time instead of disappearing like a streak, it turned round as if it was going to savage the spear. Finally Albert, the little Belgian, went down under the bobstay and drove the trident home. There was a moment of excitement and shouting, and then the fish wrenched itself clear. Even then it did not flash out of sight, but dived very slowly, moving at the same pace as the ship, until deep down under the jibboom the two blue jewels on its fins gradually dimmed and disappeared.

On the hundred and twenty-third day we had been over a fortnight creeping north through the horse latitudes at the rate of less than forty miles a day. We had been forced out to over 50° W., which is nearly the longitude of Cape Race in Newfoundland. We were not yet up to the latitude of Bermuda. With about two thousand five hundred miles to go, no sign of the westerlies, and the probability of fine summer weather, it seemed fairly certain that we should take about one hundred and forty-five days. Only a few potatoes remained, and in various other directions strict economy in food had to be observed.

Before now ships have been driven to eat a part of their cargo; on board *L'Avenir* there was a paint-mixing machine which could have been used for milling wheat. But more serious was the likelihood of a shortage of coal for the galley stove. To us personally, what mattered most was the knowledge that those waiting for us on shore would be getting anxious about the ship, since five weeks had already elapsed since we had been reported.

Day after day we had the impression of being imprisoned on an island bounded by the hard unbroken line of the horizon. For hours the ship would lie making no apparent progress, but only for a short time one evening did she completely lose steerage way, and then we were suddenly surprised to notice the Pole Star right astern. Looking from aloft the whole sea appeared speckled with sargassum weed. Deeper in the water one could see quantities of weed which had lost its buoyancy and showed a pale green colour. Having an enormous surface area the weed must sink very slowly; while perhaps in the process of decaying gas may be generated in the fronds which may give it positive buoyancy once more. As each piece of weed contains an appreciable amount of food, it was difficult to think of any reason for the great scarcity of bird life. In a week, only a few petrels and storm petrels had been sighted. Perhaps there is something stagnant about this sea to which birds as well as ships are susceptible.

Frassie was lost for a couple of days, to the captain's great distress. At last someone had an inspiration and remembered that the scuttles on the side of the main hatch had been opened for ventilation. One of these was therefore unscrewed, when out came Frassie like a shot from a gun. At least until thirst began to trouble it, an ordinary cat would have done fairly well on a plentiful diet of rats. But although he is eighteen months old, Frassie has no teeth, due, they say, to being fed on tinned salmon at too tender an age. The captain's relief was so great that a fresh tin of milk and another of salmon were immediately opened; and for the moment Frassie was none the worse. But it was rumoured that when the boys in the forecastle heard how he had been specially favoured, he would be sure to get his fur and tail pulled, if ever he ventured forward without witnesses.

Although the kitten was now over three months old and ate everything it could get including rats, Josephina still remained the complete mother, nourishing it many times a day. We supposed that having no experienced matrons to talk the matter over with, she did not know any better. She and the kitten spent hours playing together and racing about all over the ship. Sometimes Josephina got too excited and almost forgot that the kitten was not a rat. Then there was a suppressed whimper, and the kitten got a quick maternal lick before the game proceeded. It should be a fine ratter under Josephina's expert tuition.

CHAPTER XXIV

TRAINING IN SAIL

In the past it has often been claimed that our sea services produced the finest seamen in the world. More than a mere boast, this was the result of necessity. To-day it is even more vital for the Empire, now that our superiority at sea is vanishing. As the maintenance of the navy and the mercantile marine in a state of the highest efficiency affects every British man, woman and child, it has seemed right to devote a few pages to the value of sail training.

What qualities should the seamen possess? There are some which never change through the ages and which are needed every bit as much to-day as they were at the beginning of this century, when a controversy was raging around this same subject — 'Training in sail'. It was wisely said then that the fighting seaman — in war all seamen are called upon to fight — should have 'self-reliance and resource, quickness of eye and steadiness of nerve, calmness and self-possession in emergency, steadfastness in danger, helpfulness in all difficulties and a quick sense of comradeship'.

There is also that 'sea sense', which guides the seaman through doubts and anxieties to the very highest peaks of achievement, by ways which manuals of seamanship and navigation can do little to indicate, and along which regulations only form obstacles. It is generally agreed that 'sea sense' can only be acquired by being at sea, preferably in not too large a ship; it comes with experience, and like most other forms of sense, a keen power of observation will best help it to develop.

What is the result of training in a sailing vessel? Is it possible to detect any difference between these boys and others of the same age but trained in a steamship? Unfortunately it must be admitted that conclusions on these questions can only be a matter of opinion, as one cannot possibly tell what effect a different training would have had on any one person.

Many well-known seamen, who have experienced it in their young days, are against the resumption of training in sail to-day. It is possible they are giving undue consideration to the hardships and disadvantages of their young days, rather than striving to see if modern ideas can improve old methods, so that nothing good is lost and nothing useless is retained. They say that it would be a waste of time, and that, with the present day need for much technical knowledge, to learn about masts and sails is to add loads of useless lumber to already heavily burdened brains. But the sailing ship gives certain advantages in training which have not yet been reproduced in any other way.

In spite of her beauty, a sailing ship does seem to be

both artificial and unpractical in these days. Yet directly she gets to sea she becomes intensely alive and anything but futile. Once the land is left behind, the whole ship's company is welded into a solid force by the idea and determination to get the ship to the destined end of her voyage.

Safety First, that most miserable modern slogan, has no place aloft. Good seamanship and reasonable care are found to be of more use, and courage is still admired. The gear is well looked after and tested regularly: rope and other essential stores are not stinted. But the officers do not feel that, should an accident happen, every effort will be made to throw the blame on to them. The men realize that they are partly responsible for their own and each other's safety, and soon become observant, noticing any small details aloft which require attention.

In a steamship, a long voyage of ten days or a fortnight between the ports can be deadly monotonous; even a storm, provided that the ship is properly secured for sea, gives nothing but discomfort to everyone except the captain and the officers of the watch, who get the responsibility as well. In a sailing ship, the fickleness of the weather denies any possibility of monotony, and the certainty of a long voyage demands that everyone on board shall be able to contrive interest and happiness from his own resources. What is of far greater importance is the fact that the most vital part of the seaman's work in a sailing ship is done in bad weather, and while it is getting worse. Self-interest demands that the work shall be done quickly, before the increasing wind makes it harder still; to achieve this requires helpfulness to comrades and complete reliance on them for their share of it. The worse the weather, the more time is spent on deck. At night the watch on deck will be kept actually on deck constantly and will therefore absorb, besides a great deal of salt water, much valuable knowledge about the strength of the sea, the behaviour of the ship, and what she can stand.

There is also more responsibility than is evident at first. For as there is little opportunity for close supervision, bad refitting work will endanger the lives of others. So will carelessness aloft or in letting go a wrong rope. Even the helmsman is in a different position to his counterpart in a steamship, who is under the immediate eye of the officer of the watch, and can hardly make a mistake. In a sailing ship the mate on watch may be anywhere on deck superintending the work, or seeing that everything is as it should be, so that often the helmsman feels acutely alone. If a sudden squall besets the ship, the safety of the rigging may perhaps depend on his immediate and correct action.

It was most interesting to see how completely self-reliant the boys on board *L'Avenir* had become. For example, a boy of seventeen is ordered to paint down the backstays. He takes a block and the end of a rope aloft with him, coiling down enough, and stopping it with a yarn, at the cross-trees, so that he will not have the full weight of the rope as he climbs. When the block has been secured to the topgallant masthead, he reeves the rope through it, taking the end down through the forest of backstays down to the deck, where he bends on a boatswain's chair, a short piece of narrow plank slung from the corners. The chair is shackled to one of the stays so that it will slide freely up and down, then with a pot of paint slung round his waist and the hauling part of the rope gripped between his knees, the boy is ready to begin. No one supervises or watches him, and he would scorn the idea that anyone else should tend the rope to hoist or lower him.

Another typical job can be quoted. A shackle had to be put in to secure a buntline to the foot of an upper topsail. Besides telling the boy who was detailed to do it where he could find a shackle, the mate took no more interest in the work, except perhaps out of the corner of his eye to see how quickly it was done. The boy found a boatswain's chair, got a rather inadequate looking piece of two-inch rope (two inches in circumference), laid out along the yard, rove his line through the iron jackstay to which the sail is stopped, then sitting in the chair, he lowered himself down over the curve of the bellying sail until he could reach the cringle. As soon as the shackle was in, he hauled himself up to the yard, and reported to the mate as soon as all the gear was returned.

[*facing:* Changing sails on the foremast, showing the sprea⟨ for the upper back-st⟨

Discipline seems to grow on its own instead of having to be taught artificially. Everyone soon comes to recognize that the need for prompt obedience is founded on self-preservation. Punishments are rarely necessary because, although they are young and high spirited, the crew are too fully occupied to get into mischief. In the Southern Ocean while nearing Cape Horn, the chief mate's watch were slack in obeying two whistles. He therefore withdrew the privilege which they had enjoyed of remaining in the shelter of the forecastle until they were required, and made them spend the whole of their watch on deck on the fore-castle head, whatever the weather conditions were. As the nights were bitterly cold, and the punishment continued for over a week, there was no further hint of slackness.

No doubt to many people even the thought of three or four months on the high seas must be like purgatory or worse. To those liable to boredom, the experience would kill or cure. It does however provide a wonderful opportunity for independent thought or study, and yet a complete dependence on the weather prevents any feeling of monotony.

In a sailing ship devoted to training, the value is almost continuous though never irksome, for theoretical instruction and practical work can be blended judiciously. After working hours, besides looking after themselves and their clothes, the watch below inevitably learn how to amuse themselves. Poker need not be encouraged.

There would be no need to devote time for organized games, as the ship's work would provide adequate exercise. Opportunity could be given for boxing and fencing, and there is ample space on deck for a vaulting horse and horizontal bar, so that the natural urge for physical development could find outlet.

It must not be thought that any of these remarks imply criticism of the training given in Captain Gustaf Eriksson's ships. As the boys in the crew must spend about three years in sailing ships in order to become officers, there is no need for concentrated training, and the knowledge can be allowed to soak in gradually. The short-handedness of the ships makes sure that everyone will eventually get their fair share of important work, such as refitting rigging, and so on. Owing to the difficulty of competing with steamers, the crews of sailing ships must maintain them in a state of efficiency, without any help from the dockyard (dry docking excepted), which means that much time must be spent in chipping and painting.

There is one more important consideration, and that is danger. While 'Safety First' is a despicable policy which if allowed to spread unchecked will corrupt youth, and bring about the dissolution of the Empire, there is a limit to the price which can be paid for even the most desirable qualities.

Books about sailing ships are generally considered more readable if the dangers are well written up. But in practice accidents aloft are rare. Even when

Hougomont was dismasted, no one was hurt, although four men were aloft on the mizen upper topgallant yard when the mast fell. Most casualties are due to men being washed overboard while working on an open well deck. In a training ship most of this danger could be obviated by having a complete deck stretching from poop to forecastle head, which would have the additional advantage of providing ample accommodation. Occasionally a life will be lost, but at least those on board a sailing ship are secure against dangers from cars and motor bicycles.

Whenever a ship is lost at sea, the casualties are liable to be heavy. Usually the cause of the disaster has nothing to do with her motive power, though perhaps any damage to her hull may be more dangerous to a sailing ship since she may be provided with fewer separate watertight compartments than a steamer.

The sinking of the four-masted barque *Melbourne* a few years ago was especially tragic because it was so utterly unnecessary and because it occurred at the very end of a hard voyage when the lights of Queenstown were in sight, and everyone on board was thinking of the letters from home which they would be reading in a few hours' time.

Melbourne had been dogged by bad luck, for in the Atlantic on the way out to Australia she had found the SE. trades so southerly that she failed to weather the coast of South America and had to go back to the

Equator to make more easting. Then on the way home she encountered a very bad storm in the southern ocean which among other damage swept away both ladders leading down from the poop to the well-deck.

Though it was to a foreign country, there must have been a strong feeling of home-coming to those on board *Melbourne* as she passed the Fastnet and Old Head of Kinsale, and drew near to Cork Harbour. It was a clear night and her proper lights were burning. A steamer which was coming down towards her suddenly altered course, crossed successfully ahead of her, and then, to the utter dismay of those on board she altered course again and crashed into the sailing ship's port bow.

No doubt everyone was on deck to feast their eyes on the sight of land and there would not have been many casualties, only in the excitement of the collision, the captain of *Melbourne* forgot for a fatal moment the absence of the poop ladders. He fell heavily to the deck below, breaking both legs. There was no doubt that the ship was doomed, for water was pouring into the hold which had no bulkheads across it to confine the water to one end of the ship. The mates, the boatswain and some others were trying to help the captain when, only three minutes after the collision, *Melbourne* sank with the loss of eleven lives, including the captain and all those who were trying to save him.

Compared with the tragedy the explanation sounds

utterly trivial. The steamer was a big oil tanker and the young and inexperienced officer on watch lost his head and gave a wrong order to the helmsman. It was said that the captain had been on the bridge until a short time before and had only gone down because there was nothing in sight which could possibly have caused danger.

One of the A.B.'s on board *L'Avenir* had been in *Pamir* in Queenstown at the time of the disaster. He told us that most of the survivors returned to Mariehamn in *Pamir* and that they had been very badly shaken. One boy in particular was in such a nervous state that while they were among the traffic in the Skaggerack, and a steamer came fairly close he was only just prevented from jumping overboard. It was also said that the young officer of the tanker had later given in and shot himself.

CHAPTER XXV

IN THE WESTERLIES

It was not until 32° N. that we broke away from the warm embrace of the horse latitudes. When the westerlies did begin they were inclined to be fickle, varying from about NNW. to SSW.; there was only just enough weight in them to encourage the watch to brace round the yards smartly, to gain full advantage from them.

On the one hundred and twenty-seventh day, after some two months of more or less tropical conditions, there was a change which made us feel we really were approaching home. With yards squared, a fresh southwesterly breeze swelled the sails, and eight knots seemed a grand speed after such a succession of wretched runs. The water washing past our sides made lovely music. There was a summer haze over the horizon, but just enough bite in the wind to remove all cobwebs of laziness. A heavy swell rolled under us from the north-west, throwing up an occasional fountain of spray, which came pattering down on deck. A large whale escorted us for a while, showing dark blue, pale green and white when it appeared on the back of the swell. Astern of us there was a large flock of storm petrels paddling about in the wake, and darting out of the way of breaking wave crests.

Some of the old sails began to show signs of wear and a few of them had to be changed while others were simply clewed up and patched aloft from the yard. This is one of the many occasions when both hands are needed for the work. Boys who have to do the job hang well over the yard, lying on their stomachs, with their feet braced firmly aft on the footrope.

It was quite abruptly that we ran out of the Sargasso Sea, or at least out of the area where the weed is really common. Isolated pieces may be found almost anywhere in the North Atlantic, and are sometimes washed up on the shores of Great Britain.

By the next day the wind had veered round to north-west and freshened so that although nearly close hauled we made ten knots. The fore upper topsail, a veteran of eight years, split from head to foot. As there were several other holes it was decided to leave it until it went to pieces, which it would do anyhow directly an attempt was made to clew it up. It only lasted a few hours before disappearing suddenly. The watch went up at once to send down the remains. This was a day when the men aloft were not to be pitied. The sea was blue, flecked with white breaking wave tops: the bow wave broke on each side of the stem in a welter of dazzling foam, and the churned-up wake was pale green, edged with broken lines of white. A few dark cloud shadows made strange shaped islands on the water.

As the boys lay on the yards, with their feet hard braced against the footropes, the wind blew up the legs of their trousers and made the seats quiver like kites. Coats were blown up and long hair streamed away to leeward. Poor George celebrated his birthday by losing his cap which floated away like a child's balloon, accompanied by many heartfelt 'Saatans'. Though precious to him, it was a foul object, which would have made a bishop look like a dog robber.

Towards evening, black squalls followed each other at short intervals, and forced the ship over until there seemed to be no break between the leeside of the steeply sloping deck and the sea. Just before dark the mizen lower topgallant began to split, but that also was so old that it was left to die in harness. At tea the captain said that he was sure that his last ship, the *Viking*, would not be carrying royals in this weight of wind.

Some time after dark, during an especially hard squall there was a shock of a hard blow, as if a heavy sea had struck the ship's side. High over the helmsman's head and to leeward could be seen a black mass of canvas writhing against the night sky. The mizen topgallant stay had carried away near its foot and the staysail was hanging by its halyard and sheet. The stay was of three and a half inch wire, only three years old, but large staysails on these long stays put a tremendous strain on the wire, so that as the wind increases topgallant staysails are generally the first sails to come in.

Two whistles sounded almost at the same moment as the stay parted, and while the ship was being run off the wind, the jigger and the main topgallant stay-sails were lowered. By that time the mizen one, being in the lee of the topsails, had ceased behaving like a kite and was recovered without difficulty. Stays being vital if the ship is taken aback, as an immediate repair, the end of one of the mooring wires was triced up aloft, and shackled round the topgallant mast, when the lower end was rove through a block on deck and set up as taut as possible with one of the capstans.

The sixth pig was slain with some difficulty because it was fat and bad tempered, and refused at the top of its voice to come out of its sty. At last a rope was secured round it, and with someone taking in the slack round a belaying-pin a party of boys dragged it out inch by inch. After that its end was swift, and the cats, including the depraved kitten, spent most of the day crouched round a plate of raw red morsels. This pork was the first fresh meat for ten weeks. One some-times reads, in accounts of long cruises in yachts, of the difficulty of keeping fit without regular fresh food. So far, we had found nothing whatever amiss with our diet of nothing but tinned food except for potatoes, bread, cheese, dried fruits and an occasional piece of onion used for flavouring. Earlier in the voyage some of the boys did suffer from boils, but these became less frequent towards the end of the tropics.

For sheer physical fitness it would be hard to match these boys. Though they will tell you that they hardly eat anything, they are not thin; to get fat would be utterly impossible with the amount of exercise they have to take. The heavy work has some redeeming features; it is mostly corporate, hauling braces or working a capstan for example, and unless the boys are being chased by the mate on watch for being lazy, they can all feel that their work is being applied directly to getting the ship along. One much regrets the days of shanties, and wonders why some of the boys do not use them, for they all seem to know the popular ones from the gramophone records. In olden times the shanty man was as privileged and witty as a court jester, for it was his job to extemporize apt and amusing verses, full of topical interest. Most of them were of course quite unfit for polite society. If the shanty man faltered for a moment while groping for a word or idea, the rhythm was lost, and everyone cursed him for making the work seem heavier.

At dawn the next morning there was as much excitement as can be raised at that most depressing hour of the day, for right ahead of us and perhaps six miles away there was another sailing ship. She was a four-masted barque, and when it was seen that she was not carrying royals we decided at once that it must be

Viking. There was no doubt that we were coming up on her, but as soon as she realized this, up went her royal yards and thereafter we only maintained our station. In order not to lose more ground than necessary, opportunity was taken out of slight easing of the wind to change the torn mizen lower topgallant sail for a new one. This was done quite smartly, for now, since the end of the NE. trades, there were eleven in each watch, one of which was of course always at the helm. The old sail was sent down without any supervision aloft, but when the new sail was being secured to the yard, the third mate was up there with the watch.

The upper deck became a rope walk, for we had run out of spun yarn, which was required for serving over the ends of the new mizen topgallant stay. Yarns from a length of new hemp were bent together and were laid up by an emery wheel (turned by the captain) at one end and at the other end by three spindles through a plank, for twisting the yarns, turned by a board joining the three cranks, worked by Jackie. A stay has an eye spliced in the upper end which circles the mast beneath shrouds and backstays. To prevent these latter from becoming slack, the old eye of the stay was left round the mast until the end of the voyage. In the meantime a new eye could be seized over the top of the original one.

Our rival was in sight from aloft all the next day, but then came a strong south wind with torrents of

231

rain, which brought to mind the beginning of one of the summer gales of English waters. Grey curtains of rain hung round us a mile or two away, so that all day on the forecastle head a lookout stood in glistening oilskins, with thoughts reaching far beyond the range of his eyes.

While we were standing under the shelter of the boats on the bridge deck, there was a sharp crack as something struck the deck a few yards behind us. It gave one an unpleasant thrill to see a knife, with blade naked, lying on a coil of rope. One of the boys had dropped it from aloft, and later we were much amused to watch him pick it up quickly and unobtrusively, looking very ashamed, and apprehensive that the mate might have observed his lapse. In justice it must be stated that objects are very rarely dropped from aloft, though marline spikes and knives have to be used frequently. Every boy must carry one of the latter, the usual practice being to keep it in a sheath hung from the belt. Most of them have Swedish knives, murderous looking affairs, but as the voyage progressed, more variety could be observed, ranging from ladylike penknives to table-knives.

top: Changing sails. A struggle out on a yard-arm. Note the marline-spike hanging from the brace on the extreme right

bottom: Astride the end of an upper topgallant yard-arm

CHAPTER XXVI

A DOLPHIN, NEWS, AND SAILING SHIP'S CHARTERS

ONCE again Sunday, the nineteenth Sunday of the voyage, proved an eventful day, and as it was a holiday the crew were able to take advantage of it.

Early in the morning, as the weather was thick, the lookout on the forecastle head was kept busy pumping the hand fog horn, producing successions of three dismal .wails to broadcast to the damp and empty world that we were a sailing ship running free.

At breakfast time the visibility increased, and disclosed on our bow, and coming in our direction, a large oil-tanker of the usual type, with bridge amidships and funnel aft. British shares slumped once more when the Red Ensign was seen, and the ship passed by on the other side only a mile away, without altering course towards us. One heard the comment, 'damned lime-juicer', as she pushed her way towards the horizon like some bloated slug.

During the forenoon a huge school of dolphin came playing around the stem. The 'timmerman' had made a big harpoon with hinged barbs, and with a lucky strike, one of the boys sitting astride the bobstay, drove it into a seven foot animal. In a moment it was hauled up on to the forecastle-head spouting blood. It was a magnificent creature, prefectly stream-lined to a slender powerful tail with horizontal flukes. Its beak was armed with a formidable array of round sharp-pointed teeth spaced evenly in its jaws, so that when closed the teeth interlocked completely. The possession of a blowhole showed it was a mammal, but its eyes a very deep blue would have been quite enough to raise it far above the fish class. A pad was put over the spear-hole to stop the flow of blood and the creature was triced up on the forestay to be photographed. The skin was smooth and unexpectedly hard to touch, though when Frassie the cat was introduced to the animal, his claws penetrated easily, and hanging there, clasping it in his paws, he looked just as if he had caught it single-handed. After the 'springer' has been cut up, Frassie was still so angry that he would not touch any of the titbits offered to him. But when they were produced from the canvas meat safe, in which the remains of the pig was hanging, he was completely tricked, and ate them as greedily as if they had been pork.

During the afternoon the visibility increased, and a sudden shout from forward indicated another four-masted barque a few miles to the southward. The usual interminable discussions as to who she could be were settled unexpectedly quickly, though we were not able to discover whether she was the same barque that had been in sight ahead of us a few days previously.

We were still watching her intently, when through the clearing mist came a steamer which circled round her, and then to our intense delight came towards us. As she approached the third mate was busy preparing and hoisting the flag signal 'What is the longitude?' for with sudden alterations of temperature and climate there is always the possibility that the chronometers may change their rate. Apart from that the English Channel in June is notorious for fogs, so that accuracy of navigation is vital.

British shares soared as the Red Ensign was made out, flying from her stern. She was the *Mopan* of Liverpool, belonging to Fyffe's, presumably bound for the West Indies for a load of bananas.

The captain gave us permission to ask by semaphore 'any news?'

Back came the reply, 'Max Baer beat Carnera.'

We could not help laughing, though not many people could give enough world news in a few words, to satisfy a ship's crew of many different nationalities, who have been cut off from the world for over four months.

Luckily the *Mopan's* courtesy was inexhaustible, for she circled round us, passing so close that a short megaphone conversation could be held.

'What sailing ship is that?' we shouted.

'*Archibald Russell*.'

'Any more news?'

'Australian Test team beat England.'

'We are one hundred and thirty days out.'

'There is no news of international importance.'

'Is the King all right?'

'Yes, quite.'

'Thank you very much for giving us the news.'

'Two sailing ships have already arrived. *Parma* about a fortnight ago, and *Passat* is at Dublin after a passage of one hundred and sixteen days. We will report you to Lloyd's to-night.'

Apart from the relief of knowing our longitude was only ten minutes out, her interest in us gave untold pleasure. If unanimous good wishes can accomplish anything, she should have made a very successful passage.

'Her skipper has been in sailing ships,' said the sail-maker, 'he is no tramcar conductor.'

As every sailing ship carries a miniature League of Nations, it would appreciably enhance our prestige if British shipowners would encourage their masters to take every opportunity of speaking the sailing ships they may meet. A fair proportion of the steamers we have sighted could have come within signalling distance at an extra cost of only a few shillings. But in these days of keen competition and unimaginative office staffs, searching through logs and engine-room registers for halfpennies, many masters dare not deviate a mile from their course.

In case we should become proud, the captain took care to point out that the only news we should get from a British ship would of course be about sport. He has a particular dislike for cricket because, when last he was at Port Lincoln, the agent there said he could not see about their loading that day, because he was playing in a cricket match. The captain explained that in Scandinavia only young people bother much about ball games. It tickles him immensely to think of respectable elderly gentlemen devoting their retirement to hitting a little white ball.

The cook would probably have liked to roast the boy who caught the 'springer', for it gave him a great deal of extra work. The meat from the dolphin's back, after being soaked in salt water and vinegar for twenty-four hours, was made with flour, pepper, and salt, into fish balls about the size of a small hen's egg. They were dark, were served in a thick gravy, and tasted just like rissoles, without the slightest suspicion of fishiness. The cook made eight hundred of them on a basis of twenty-five for each member of the crew. The evening meal must have been something of an orgy, for, as the penultimate pig had been slaughtered that day, there were also blood pancakes and liver pudding. The latter is made into a sort of cottage pie, the liver being cut up small and mixed with rice and raisins.

Having been installed when she was a cadet ship, the galley range is much too large and is far from economical. The result has brought on a coal crisis so that for the last few weeks the cook has been cut down to a quarter of his usual allowance. All the available wood, over a ton altogether, had already been burned.

When we were still six or seven hundred miles from Falmouth, the charm of the voyage gave way to regrets that it was so nearly over. When there was a good sailing breeze one's chief thought was that we should arrive too quickly. The uncertainty of what the future had in store for us strove with the desire for news, and the longing to see the myriad different greens of the English summer. Anxiety about possible events that might have taken place while we were away, made us dread the first contact with the telegraph line.

One could feel that each individual's thoughts about the land were having an effect on the spirit of the ship. From being united to one end, our different private interests were becoming more important than the ship and her work. It is very sad to come across anyone to whom home-coming means nothing, or worse still is actually distasteful. Some of these boys, who have led men's lives for one, two or three years, know that at home they will be thought of and treated as children. The boy who was suffering from T.B. got into a terrible state of distress because he dreaded breaking the news of his illness to his parents, whose hope is in his future.

Most of the boys were looking forward most intensely to getting the mail, though one or two said that they only expected a couple of letters, even after four and a half months.

Besides coal, there were other shortages in more or less important directions. The captain had already divided up all the cigarettes that remained in his slop chest, among any of the crew who wanted them. No doubt those who did well at poker retailed their winnings back to the losers at 'sea price'. Supplies of pipe tobacco were almost exhausted, and on the captain's recommendation one of the hardy mariners aft blended teased-out manila rope yarns with what little he had left. One could not deny that it smoked, but the patient said that it gave him a somewhat airy, other-worldly sensation. The captain further suggested that when he had got well run-in on manila, he should change gradually to tarred hemp, which undoubtedly has more body in it. Fortunately there were not many pipe-smokers on board, otherwise one could picture all the ropes getting shorter and shorter, until the yards could not be braced round, and finally, as the halyards disappeared in smoke, it would be impossible to lower the sails at all.

With a pig still in hand and a fresh westerly breeze blowing, there was no longer any need for rigid economy of food, and meals resumed normal proportions, except for a shortage of potatoes.

About this time a tragedy occurred which hit the captain very hard. Frassie, his favourite cat, disappeared. As he had been missing all day, in the evening some of the watch on deck, assisted by the steward and his boy armed with bunches of keys, made a complete search of the ship, looking into hatches, all cupboards and storerooms. There was no sign of him anywhere, and we suspected that he had been a victim of foul play. Having been round the Horn twice, it seemed most unlikely that he would fall overboard in calm weather. Someone may have grudged the amount of pork that Frassie consumed.

A sailing ship's charter with a wheat cargo stipulates as a rule that the port of destination shall be any European one outside the Mediterranean. While on its way from Australia each cargo may be re-sold many times, but from the moment the ship which carries it reaches Falmouth or Queenstown, the owners of the cargo may only keep her there for a week without paying demurrage before informing her of the port of discharge. Falmouth and Queenstown are chosen as the ports for orders as they have large sheltered bays where there are no harbour dues, and which can be entered and left without incurring heavy charges for tugs.

The usual unloading ports are London, Liverpool, Cardiff, Belfast, Dublin, Hull, or Glasgow, but occasionally a ship may go to Avonmouth or to Ipswich. London is probably the most popular port, and as a matter of course the crews will visit the famous Charlie Brown's; the young Scandinavians consider Limehouse a bad and dangerous locality, in which they are safe only when inside the dock gates.

In 1933, *L'Avenir* unloaded at Avonmouth and found it a most pleasantly hospitable place; a number of those on board were taken out to see something of the English countryside for the first time, and appreciated it greatly. The seaman's life in an English port is often a miserable one, for talkies are less satisfactory for a foreigner than silent pictures, and public-houses are liable to be closed when most needed. We were sometimes asked why in England there were no decent clean cafés with music of sorts, where a man could take his wife or friend to pass the evening, without the need for spending more than the price of some beer or coffee. The only answer was the not very helpful one that in England, the home was the place where people preferred to pass their spare time, and to entertain their friends; and that probably it was more common to visit other homes in England than in continental countries. The public-house is the only refuge for visitors, and for those whose houses are not comfortable enough for anything but meals and sleep.

It was at Avonmouth that a small girl of fourteen became so attached to *L'Avenir* that she spent every possible day on board, helping the cook or steward, and trying to persuade the captain to take her as an apprentice. It was not just a passing craze, for she wrote to the latter while he was in Australia, urging him to promise her a berth on the next voyage.

It makes all the difference in the world if the harbour-master of the unloading port has himself served in sailing ships. It is as good as being given the freedom of the port, and harbour regulations can be stretched to breaking point. From time to time the harbour master will bring a party of friends to see over the ship, telling them heroic great lies about life in the southern ocean and off Cape Horn, which the captain and mates support with loyalty and even admiration.

At some ports, powerful machinery sucks the wheat out of the holds in an incredibly short space of time. It takes longer in sailing ship than a steamer, as the stevedores must cut the stitching at the mouth of each bag, and empty it into the central pool, into which the trunk of the machine is thrust. The suction is tremendously powerful, for hats, empty bags and shirts are liable to disappear for ever, and they say that the machine would not be above taking trousers as well, if one were to get too close to the business end.

Customs formalities, restrictions and petty annoyances vary greatly all the world over. In some South American ports the visiting officials must be handed quietly eight or ten pounds in an envelope, or else they will carry out a minute search until they find somewhere, perhaps among the private possessions of the crew, some trifling object which has not been declared on the manifest. Then the heaviest penalties are exacted.

In Australia a foreign ship may not use any of her own stores unless duty is paid on them. From the crew's point of view this may have the advantage of getting them more fresh food purchased from local sources than they might otherwise have. But it is irksome that the sailmaker is unable to make new sails with canvas from Dundee, unless a heavy duty is paid. No canvas of good enough quality is made in Australia, so the sailmaker is employed repairing old sails, or using canvas which has been cut up before reaching port. In some places the captain must produce receipted bills for food bought ashore. In others the ship's cat has a price of fifty pounds on its head, or rather the ship would be fined that amount, should the cat elect to take up its residence ashore. Let us hope its paw-print is taken, otherwise the law might be broken as it is regularly by Chinese, who return to China, and sell their passports to someone else, who could not otherwise enter Australia under the present immigration laws.

In the United Kingdom, visiting ships have only their liquor and tobacco sealed up during their stay in port, though they may be searched for drugs.

CHAPTER XXVII

THE END OF THE VOYAGE

It was during the afternoon of the one hundred and thirty-seventh day, when we were some two hundred miles from Scilly Islands, that we reached the Continental slope; in a run of only a few miles the depth changed from two miles to less than a quarter of a mile. The sea appeared to change colour, but one could not be certain whether this was due to changing weather conditions or to a greater wealth of plant life in the water. Other indications that we were approaching land were not lacking. Towards evening several gannets passed by on their way shorewards, some of them first circling once round the ship in a friendly way. After dark we saw the lights of several steam trawlers, which reminded the captain that once when he was in *Lawhill* to the north of Scotland, a trawler closed them to within heaving-line distance and exchanged a quantity of fish for a couple of bottles of Schnapps. Hours later, in the middle of the night, the same trawler reappeared, and tipsy shouts came across the dark water inviting them to a further barter.

Trawlers usually work in depth up to one hundred fathoms, though some of the larger craft fish for hake on the Continental slope, in depths of from two hundred to three hundred fathoms; they have occasionally gone as deep as five hundred fathoms, over half a mile. Trawlers are generally from one hundred and twenty to one hundred and sixty feet long, and can be distinguished from drifters by the four 'gallows', or large iron frames, which are placed forward and aft on each side, to which the otter boards are hoisted, when the net is hauled up for emptying.

L'Avenir's unnatural passion for calms was not to be satisfied without a final two days' struggle against baffling breezes, which playfully headed us before they dropped away to nothing, leaving the ship going round slowly in circles. Several times it seemed as if we might have to make for Queenstown. But the captain never gave up Falmouth as his objective, remembering the sad case of another master who sailed from Norway for Australia and first decided to go down through the Channel. Meeting head winds in the southern part of the North Sea, he thought it best to go north round Scotland after all. When the ship was back again off Norway, the wind came from the north-west, which sent her flying down towards the Channel once again. This went on regularly, and the captain changed his mind so often that, after sixty days, being then close to Ireland, he deemed it prudent to put into port for more provisions. He got the sack as well. Other ships that left Europe at the same time were in Australia in eighty odd days.

Quite suddenly when about seventy miles from the

Scilly Islands, we heard the homely cries of seagulls, and found a flock of lesser blackbacked gulls wheeling around us, with one skua among them. Gulls have no right to be considered deep-water birds for most of the species are longshore loafers, rarely going far from land. The kittiwake is the only one which makes a habit of following ships for long distances.

After an hour's heavy rain, several homing pigeons adopted the ship as a temporary resting place. Two that insisted on strutting about the deck were caught to save them from the cat; they were safely housed for the night, given water, bread and wheat, and were released the following morning with messages giving our position and date. One of them belonged to a federation in Durham, and had probably been competing in a race from France. We hoped we should not be blamed for tampering with the field. Anyhow, these pigeons were hopeless 'also rans', for when they were released they only flew a couple of times round the ship, before settling comfortably on a royal yard.

After dark there were ships all round us, for we were close to one of the main focal points of the world's sea traffic. But we could not get anyone to answer our flashing signals asking for a weather report.

Midsummer's day was no advertisement for the English climate; it was cold, with occasional rain and the usual fine intervals of a few minutes, but there was no steady breeze. Sunday's rest was constantly broken by having to brace round the yards, and tack or wear.

[facing: 'Land in sig

The following dawn a huge German liner tore past us a few miles off, and a little later the smart looking French liner *Lafayette* came very close to us, courteously signalling by flags that we were thirty-three miles from Bishop Rock, the tall lighthouse marking the western edge of the Scilly Islands.

During the afternoon we saw from aloft the low outlines of the Scillies themselves, the first land we had sighted since leaving Australia. Though everyone went up to catch a glimpse of the land, there was less excitement than a longing for all the things we had missed during the slow months of the voyage.

A patch of sunlight shining on the Bishop Rock lighthouse made it look like a slender church spire. Gulls wheeled and squawked over the mast heads. Some orange peel floated past. We were almost home.

In the afternoon an exhibition of models was held on the forecastle; there were five of *L'Avenir* and two galleons. Some of the boys had used wonderful ingenuity; one had made the teak rail which runs round the ship out of bristles from a deck scrubber.

On the last day of the voyage there was so much of interest to be seen, that it was only occasionally that one realized with a wave of sadness, how intensely happy we had been. At dawn the four-masted barque *Passat* was seen standing down ahead of us, having passed between the Scillies and Land's End. She was homeward bound, and must have taken in the bare minimum of ballast at her unloading port, for even with the light northerly breeze she was not carrying royals.

The Scilly Islands were in sight to the northward of us, but too far off to distinguish anything but the lighthouses and St. Martin's daymark, so we had to content ourselves with memories stimulated by the chart. We could just see Annet, the island where the puffins and shearwaters nest in holes, while hungry great blackbacked gulls lie in wait just above. The very names of the rocks have a romantic ring about them. Crim rocks, Retarrier Ledge, Great and Little Minalto, Menpingrim, Tearing Ledges, Great Wingletang, Illiswilgig, Hellweathers, and the Crebinicks. Many of these have provided wealth for the Scilly Islanders in the days when wrecks were looked forward to as heaven-sent. There is a story that during service one Sunday morning, news came into the church that a fine ship was ashore not far away. The congregation was about to rush out when the parson shouted from the pulpit: 'Wait a moment, brethren, until I have got my surplice off and then we'll all start square.'

One could easily imagine that the old days had come back, for while *Passat* was still in sight to the south, we saw from aloft the sails of two more barques. They were well to the northward, having evidently made for Queenstown until the wind went northerly. All around us were the homely brown sails of Brixham trawlers.

Perhaps the best thrill came with the sighting of the

high moors near Lands End. A little later on, a cruiser, H.M.S. *Effingham*, came down channel, and at 4 p.m. in accordance with time-honoured custom, she exercised the recovery of a man overboard. We saw a puff of smoke come out of her funnels as she stopped and went astern, while her two sea boats were lowered and raced each other to recover the lifebuoys dropped close to the imaginary man.

The tidal stream flooding up the Channel helped us on our way, so that soon we slipped past Porth Gwarra, Mousehole, Newlyn, Penzance, and St. Michael's Mount until we reached the Lizard. It was here that we got the first real scent of Cornish earth, while high overhead above the gulls, swallows shrieked a welcome while they chased insects blown off the land.

Before reaching the Manacles, we saw a fourth barque which had evidently just left Falmouth after receiving her orders. The first direct link with the shore was a dirty looking Falmouth quay punt with her mast cut down to a mere stump, a noisy engine and a beery-looking crew of two, '*Good* evening, Captain, you've made a fine passage,' opened a conversation which soon degenerated into a flow of whining requests to be employed as ship's boat.

Next came the cheerful little pilot.

'England has won the second Test . . .'

'£28,000,000 surplus in the budget . . .'

'All the big yachts are in Falmouth . . .'

'The *Abraham Ryndberg* made the shortest passage so far and came by the Cape of Good Hope . . .'

'The *Ponape* and the *Archibald Russell* have been reported off the Lizard.'

The news that comforted us most was that all the other sailing ships had made slow passages, so that we were not in any disgrace.

The pilot gave us a handful of Sunday papers, and we took a quick glance at the headlines for the most important news. We got it.

'Police know Trunk Murderer'

'Drama in Locked Bungalow'

'Larwood . . .'

We were home at last.

As dusk was falling we crept slowly up towards the lighthouse on St. Anthony's Point. No whistle was needed to summon the hands, for everyone was on deck. Royals, upper and lower top gallants were furled in succession, next the courses and lower topsails, then as the ship rounded up to the wind, the staysails came rattling down the stays.

'All right,' shouted the pilot from the forecastle, 'she has lost her way.'

'Let go,' answered the captain.

After a second's pause there came the heavy splash of the anchor, followed by the roar of the chain cable running out.

Suddenly there was a cheer, and in a moment cheers were spreading quickly along the deck, being echoed by the boys high up and only faintly visible along the yards.

The voyage was over. Turn over the page.

BIBLIOGRAPHY

BIBLIOGRAPHY

The Ocean	SIR JOHN MURRAY
Findlay's Directory of the South Pacific Ocean	
Birds of the Ocean	W. B. ALEXANDER
The Seas	F. S. RUSSELL and C. M. YOUNGE
South American Pilot. Part I	(British Admiralty)
Findlay's Directory of the North Pacific Ocean	
A Voyage Round the World in the years 1740-1744	LORD ANSON

255

3,

17 M Eliot
5' Wool